REVOLUTIONARY SOCIAL TRANSFORMATION

Critical Studies in Education and Culture Series

Naming the Multiple: Poststructuralism and Education
Michael Peters, editor

Literacy in the Library:
Negotiating the Spaces Between Order and Desire
Mark Dressman

Thinking Again: Education After Postmodernism
Nigel Blake, Paul Smeyers, Richard Smith, and Paul Standish

Racial Categorization of Multiracial Children in Schools
Jane Ayers Chiong

bell hooks' Engaged Pedagogy:
Education for Critical Consciousness
Namulundah Florence

Wittgenstein: Philosophy, Postmodernism, Pedagogy
Michael Peters and James Marshall

Policy, Pedagogy, and Social Inequality:
Community College Student Realities in Post-Industrial America
Penelope E. Herideen

Psychoanalysis and Pedagogy
Stephen Appel, editor

The Rhetoric of Diversity and the Traditions of American
Literary Study: Critical Multiculturalism in English
Lesliee Antonette

Becoming and Unbecoming White:
Owning and Disowning a Racial Identity
Christine Clark and James O'Donnell

Critical Pedagogy: An Introduction, 2nd Edition
Barry Kanpol

Michel Foucault: Materialism and Education
Mark Olssen

REVOLUTIONARY SOCIAL TRANSFORMATION

Democratic Hopes, Political Possibilities and Critical Education

Paula Allman

Foreword by
Peter McLaren

Critical Studies in Education and Culture Series
Edited by Henry A. Giroux

Bergin & Garvey
Westport, Connecticut • London

Copyright Acknowledgments

Pedagogy of the Oppressed, by Paulo Freire, translated by Myra Bergman Ramos, © Copyright 1970, 1993, by Paulo Freire, extracts reprinted by permission of The Continuum Publishing Company and by permission of Penguin Books.

Karl Marx: Selected Writings, edited by David McLellan, 1977, extracts reprinted by permission of Oxford University Press.

Selections from the Prison Notebooks, by Antonio Gramsci, edited and translated by Quintin Hoare and Geoffrey Nowell Smith, London 1971, extracts reprinted by permission of Lawrence & Wishart.

Library of Congress Cataloging-in-Publication Data

Allman, Paula,
Revolutionary social transformation : democratic hopes, political possibilities and critical education / Paula Allman ; foreword by Peter McLaren.
p. cm.—(Critical studies in education and culture series, ISSN 1064–8615)
Includes bibliographical references and index.
ISBN 0–89789–667–X (alk. paper)—0–89789–803–6 (pbk. : alk. paper)
1. Social change. 2. Democracy. 3. Equality. 4. Sustainable development. 5. Consciousness. I. Title. II. Series.
HM831.A45 1999
303.4—dc21 99–14843

British Library Cataloguing in Publication Data is available.

Library of Congress Catalog Card Number: 99–14843
ISBN: 0–89789–803–6 (pbk.)
ISSN: 1064–8615

First published in 1999

Bergin & Garvey, 88 Post Road West, Westport, CT 06881
An imprint of Greenwood Publishing Group, Inc.
www.greenwood.com

Printed in the United States of America

The paper used in this book complies with the Permanent Paper Standard issued by the National Information Standards Organization (Z39.48–1984).

P

In order to keep this title in print and available to the academic community, this edition was produced using digital reprint technology in a relatively short print run. This would not have been attainable using traditional methods. Although the cover has been changed from its original appearance, the text remains the same and all materials and methods used still conform to the highest book-making standards.

For Chris (Becky) and Tigs

Contents

Series Foreword

Educational reform has fallen upon hard times. The traditional assumption that schooling is fundamentally tied to the imperatives of citizenship designed to educate students to exercise civic leadership and public service has been eroded. The schools are now the key institution for producing professional, technically trained, credentialized workers for whom the demands of citizenship are subordinated to the vicissitudes of the marketplace and the commercial public sphere. Given the current corporate and right wing assault on public and higher education, coupled with the emergence of a moral and political climate that has shifted to a new Social Darwinism, the issues which framed the democratic meaning, purpose, and use to which education might aspire have been displaced by more vocational and narrowly ideological considerations.

The war waged against the possibilities of an education wedded to the precepts of a real democracy is not merely ideological. Against the backdrop of reduced funding for public schooling, the call for privatization, vouchers, cultural uniformity, and choice, there are the often ignored larger social realities of material power and oppression. On the national level, there has been a vast resurgence of racism. This is evident in the passing of anti-immigration laws such as Proposition 187 in California, the dismantling of the welfare state, the demonization of black youth that is taking place in the popular media, and the remarkable attention provided by the media to forms of race talk that argue for the intellectual inferiority of blacks or dismiss calls for racial justice as simply a holdover from the "morally bankrupt" legacy of the 1960s.

Poverty is on the rise among children in the United States, with 20 percent of all children under the age of eighteen living below the poverty line. Unemployment is growing at an alarming rate for poor youth of color, especially in the urban centers. While black youth are policed and disciplined in and out of the nation's schools, conservative and liberal educators define education through the ethically limp discourses of privatization, national standards, and global competitiveness.

Many writers in the critical education tradition have attempted to challenge the right wing fundamentalism behind educational and social reform in both the United States and abroad while simultaneously providing ethical signposts for a public discourse about education and democracy that is both prophetic and transformative. Eschewing traditional categories, a diverse number of critical theorists and educators have successfully exposed the political and ethical implications of the cynicism and despair that has become endemic to the discourse of schooling and civic life. In its place, such educators strive to provide a language of hope that inextricably links the struggle over schooling to understanding and transforming our present social and cultural dangers.

At the risk of overgeneralizing, both cultural studies theorists and critical educators have emphasized the importance of understanding theory as the grounded basis for "intervening into contexts and power . . . in order to enable people to act more strategically in ways that may change their context for the better."[1] Moreover, theorists in both fields have argued for the primacy of the political by calling for and struggling to produce critical public spaces, regardless of how fleeting they may be, in which "popular cultural resistance is explored as a form of political resistance."[2] Such writers have analyzed the challenges that teachers will have to face in redefining a new mission for education, one that is linked to honoring the experiences, concerns, and diverse histories and languages that give expression to the multiple narratives that engage and challenge the legacy of democracy.

Equally significant is the insight of recent critical educational work that connects the politics of difference with concrete strategies for addressing the crucial relationships between schooling and the economy, and citizenship and the politics of meaning in communities of multicultural, multiracial, and multilingual schools.

Critical Studies in Education and Culture attempts to address and demonstrate how scholars working in the fields of cultural studies and the critical pedagogy might join together in a radical project and practice informed by theoretically rigorous discourses that affirm the critical but refuse the cynical, and establish hope as central to a critical pedagogical and political practice but eschew a romantic utopianism. Central to such a project is the issue of how pedagogy might provide cultural studies theorists and educators with an opportunity to engage in pedagogical practices that are not only transdisciplinary, transgressive, and oppositional, but also connected to a wider project designed to further racial, economic, and political democracy.[3] By taking seriously the relations between culture and power, we further the possibilities of resistance, struggle, and change.

Critical Studies in Education and Culture is committed to publishing work that opens a narrative space that affirms the contextual and the specific while simultaneously recognizing the ways in which such spaces are shot through with issues of power. The series attempts to continue an important legacy of theoretical work in cultural studies in which related debates on pedagogy are understood and addressed within the larger context of social responsibility, civic courage, and the reconstruction of democratic public life. We must keep in mind Raymond Williams's insight that the "deepest impulse (informing cultural politics) is the desire to make learning part of the process of social change itself."[4] Education as a cultural pedagogical practice takes place across multiple sites, which include not only schools and universities but also the mass media, popular culture, and other public spheres, and signals how within diverse contexts, education makes us both subjects of and subject to relations of power.

This series challenges the current return to the primacy of market values and simultaneous retreat from politics so evident in the recent work of educational theorists, legislators, and policy analysts. Professional relegitimation in a troubled time seems to be the order of the day as an increasing number of academics both refuse to recognize public and higher education as critical public spheres and offer little or no resistance to the ongoing vocationalization of schooling, the continuing evisceration of the intellectual labor force, and the current assaults on the working poor, the elderly, and women and children.[5]

Emphasizing the centrality of politics, culture, and power, *Critical Studies in Education and Culture* will deal with pedagogical issues that contribute in imaginative and transformative ways to our understanding of how critical knowledge, democratic values, and social practices can provide a basis for teachers, students, and other cultural workers to redefine their role as engaged and public intellectuals. Each volume will attempt to rethink the relationship between language and experience, pedagogy and human agency, and ethics and social responsibility as part of a larger project for engaging and deepening the prospects of democratic schooling in a multiracial and multicultural society. *Critical Studies in Education and Culture* takes on the responsibility of witnessing and addressing the most pressing problems of public schooling and civic life, and engages culture as a crucial site and strategic force for productive social change.

Henry A. Giroux

NOTES

1. Lawrence Grossberg, "Toward a Genealogy of the State of Cultural Studies," in Cary Nelson and Dilip Parameshwar Gaonkar, eds., *Disciplinarity and Dissent in Cultural Studies* (New York: Routledge, 1996), p. 143.

2. David Bailey and Stuart Hall, "The Vertigo of Displacement," *Ten 8*, 2:3 (1992), 19.

3. My notion of transdisciplinary comes from Mas'ud Zavarzadeh and Donald Morton, "Theory, Pedagogy, Politics: The Crisis of the 'Subject' in the Humanities," in Mas'ud Zavarzadeh and Donald Morton, eds., *Theory Pedagogy Politics: Texts for Change* (Urbana, IL: University of Illinois Press, 1992), p. 10. At issue here is neither ignoring the boundaries of discipline-based knowledge nor simply fusing different disciplines, but creating theoretical paradigms, questions, and knowledge that cannot be taken up within the policed boundaries of the existing disciplines.

4. Raymond Williams, "Adult Education and Social Change," in *What I Came to Say* (London: Hutchinson-Radus, 1989), p. 158.

5. The term "professional legitimation" comes from a personal correspondence with Professor Jeff Williams of East Carolina University.

Foreword

Many mysteries lie buried in the Secret Museum of the Human Race surrounding the durability of human misery and why it has been permitted to persist for so long over the centuries. For generations upon generations, philosophers, theologians, social theorists, urban planners—for that matter, individuals from nearly all walks of life—have attempted in some measure to solve this mystery. Few thinkers have been able to explore the depths of this mystery with more success than Karl Marx. It is the social theory of Karl Marx—especially his revolutionary theory of consciousness—that serves as the centerpiece of this new book by Paula Allman.

Revolutionary Social Transformation occurs against the backdrop—at least within the academic precincts of the North American academy—of a widespread reluctance on the part of the new educational left to engage in serious Marxist analysis, beyond the baleful farrago of assertions that Marx and his heirs have sunk into a "solidarity of defeat" in the wake of advanced capitalist society. The delinquent desire that lures capital to the four corners of the earth in search of profit at all costs appears to have ushered in a permanent victory for the forces of accumulation. To bring Marx back to the realm of the living appears to require a salvage operation on the momentous scale of raising the *Titanic* from the murky floor of the Atlantic. The belligerents—known as communists and socialists—continue to be rubbished by the "victors" of history and consigned to the ocean floor to scuttle about from rock to rock in search of a new theory. Thirty years after those fiery days of May 1968, when students, the working-class, clerks and technicians joined the general strike and marched through the streets of Paris in a quest for the "totally other," the legacy of Marx seems sealed in despair. Bertell Ollman notes that many socialists "have reacted to this recent turn of history by questioning whether any form of socialism is possible" (1998, p. 342). What has resulted, according to Ollman, is a type of "future shyness" that one sees in the writings of many members of the left today. But there are signs that this situation may be changing. And the epochal shift in global capitalism may be one of the reasons. As long as capitalism seemed to be "in charge," a strong case could be made for the "end of history" thesis. However, once capitalism began to suffer a series of serious afflictions in Asia, in Latin America and in Russia, then a case could be made that Marx was indeed a prophet after all.

Capitalism continues to mutate. In today's informational economy, there no longer exists the dependence on large agglomerations of hands-on labor power as in traditional manufacturing. In an information economy, it is much more difficult for labor to bargain with capital and win political rights (Kundnani, 1998/1999). Neoliberal economic and social reform is afoot today, grounded in a firm belief that the global economy is an obdurate, inevitable and historically permanent condition. Yet that confidence is beginning to erode.

Eric Hobsbawm describes the neoliberal perspective as underwritten by a consensus of neoclassical academic economists

> who dream of a nirvana of an optimally efficient and frictionless economy of a self-adjusting global market, that is to say an economy with minimal interference by states or other insitutions. Given the state of the world, this implied a systematic policy of privatizing and deregulating the economy. . . . Theirs is economics without political, social or any other non-mathematical dimension. In practice, of course, it is an economics which fitted the economy of transnational corporations and other operators in a period of boom. This consensus is now at an end. [1998, p. 5]

Inequality and maldistribution abounds, as the global economy deregulation, the segmentation of the market, the shrinking labor market and permanent underemployment and unemployment create a world of vast and inexorable polarization. Hobsbawm captures this situation—as it pertains to Western metropoles—with a candidness worth repeating:

What is happening today—and in the absence of unions and government action, without any countervailing forces—is what we see in the world cities like London and New York which are the hubs of the global economy: a polarisation between a concentration of high-income-generating jobs in high-profit-making firms (finance, media) and a low-wage, casual, service population—between the city dealers and the office cleaners and security staff, catering workers etc. Let us leave aside the socially obscene extremes of seven-figure salaries which corporation executives vote each other, insisting that they express their market scarcity, and the stratospheric rewards for the top showbiz handful—rock stars, football stars, premier league clubs etc compared to the rest. (Actually it has produced a crazy situation where wealthy individuals—not corporations—have more money to spend on politics than national parties, or even poorer states.) The major tendency in the developed countries is to produce a division between the highly qualified or specialized and the low-skilled. The consumer economy is equally polarising: stratospherically priced *Vogue* fashion confronts Oxfam shop second-hand clothes. The middle ground is being squeezed—whether in the form of middle incomes or modestly profitable, but otherwise entirely viable, firms. [1998, p. 8]

Robert Brenner (1998) notes that outside the United States and Europe, the international economy is experiencing an economic downturn that is more severe than any that has occurred since the 1930s. The left consensus that the growing economic turmoil that is also engulfing Europe and North America is mainly a crisis linked to the irresponsibility of short-term investment is woefully short-sighted. Brenner argues that the rise of finance capital and of neoliberalism is not really the cause of the current international economic crisis as much as it is a result of such a crisis. Brenner links the cause of the current economic crisis to the growth of overcapacity and overproduction leading to the falling profitability in manufacturing that began in the late 1960s. Neoliberalism and monetarism resulted from the failure of Keynesian deficit spending to restore profitability and reignite capital accumulation. At this current historical conjuncture, however, it is becoming more in doubt, even to many conservatives, that the the principle of free-market allocation per se will always bring about the best possible conditions. According to Brenner, what is needed is a society built upon the principles of socialism and democratic social control over the economy from the bottom up by the working classes.

Because he believes that the current stage of capitalism is characterized by far greater complexity and much faster change and interaction than at any time in human history, Bertell Ollman argues that a dialectical understanding of social life is "more indispensable now than ever before" (1998, p. 342). He articulates a dialectical method that he breaks down into six successive moments. The ontological moment has to do with the infinite number of mutually dependent processes that make up the totality or structured whole of social life. The epistemological moment deals with how to organize thinking in order to understand such a world, abstracting out the main patterns of change and interaction. The moment of inquiry appropriates the patterns of these internal relationships in order to further the project of investigation. The moment of intellectual reconstruction or self-clarification puts together the results of such an investigation for oneself. The moment of exposition entails describing to a particular audience the dialectical grasp of the facts by taking into account how others think. Finally, the moment of praxis uses the clarification of the facts of social life to consciously act in and on the world, changing it while also deepening one's understanding of it simultaneously. These dialectical acts, which are traversed repeatedly over time, bear a striking similarity to the thought of Antonio Gramsci and the pedagogy of Paulo Freire.

In her discussion of Freire and Gramsci, it becomes clear that Paula Allman is in full agreement with Brenner's recommendation. Her book is a story about the struggle for critical consciousness read against the powerful dialectical contradictions of capitalism that exist between productive labor and capital and between production and exchange and their historical development. While to a large extent the guiding narratives of this book concern the politics of interpreting revolutionary theory, it is also an immensely personal story of Allman's own journey toward critical consciousness through her engagement with the writings of Marx, Freire and Gramsci.

The linchpin of Allman's analysis is Marx's theory of consciousness/praxis. For Allman, this theory marks both an epistemological and an ontological revolution in the way that we think about "knowledge" and "being" and the relationship between them. Emphasizing the importance of a critical/dialectical praxis that is infused with an alternative educational approach—one that can be applied in both formal and informal contexts—Allman reveals how critical praxis needs to employ both cultural action and cultural revolution. Freire and Gramsci share with Marx the idea that our human potential is directly linked to human relationships in naturally occurring circumstances—that is, in lived experiences. Gramsci also shares with Freire Marx's notion that there are different types or levels of consciousness: for instance, common sense, ideology and the philosophy of praxis. For Gramsci, the philosophy of praxis represents "the pinnacle of philosophical achievement" and provides a scientific, nonideological and dialectical coherence. The philosophy of praxis is a radical educational praxis, a method of analysis and a conception of the world that involves a dialectical analysis of reality and a dialectical unity with the people. It involves making coherent the principles and problems of the masses in their practical activity. According to Allman, Gramsci advocates the same sort of changed relationship to knowledge and transformed relations between teachers and students as does Freire. And while Allman stresses the indebtedness of Freire and Gramsci to Marx, she writes, too, about how Freire and Gramsci also contribute something new to Marx's thought with their concept of how cultural workers should work with people prior to the moment of revolution and with a very specific idea of alliance building.

Ultimately, Allman's book has implications about re-thinking and recreating democracy through the development of collective or communal concepts of rights and responsibilities and for putting technology into the service of integrating or reintegrating the political with the economic realms of collective decision-making and popular democractic governance. Her challenge to relativism engages four types of truth: metatranshistorical truths, transhistorical truth, historically specific truth and conjuncturally specific truth.

Allman rescues Freire's work from the reformists who wish to limit his legacy to its contribution to consciousness-raising. Reformists are often victims of "subjectivism" that occurs when people verbally denounce social injustice but leave intact the existing structure of society. Allman emphasizes that Freire's approach only makes sense when read in the context of Marx's negative concept of ideology and the epistemological and ontological shifts that his approach requires.

In her clear and convincing explanation of the dialectical contradictions of the capitalist economy, and her dedication to both cultural action and cultural revolution, Allman also offers us, in *Revolutionary Social Transformation*, a serious challenge to certain trajectories of postmodernist theory, with its enthrallment toward open-endedness, its resistance to fixity and its quest for flexible identities. It calls attention to the bourgeois outlawry, fashionable philistinism and aristocratic brigandism that characterizes those forms of postmodern criticism that betray a civil inattention to issues of relations of production and a motivated amnesia toward history.

Allman warns that a limited praxis—a praxis that does not take into account the totality of social relations—only reproduces the given social order or dialectical contradictions in their inversion. Allman shows how revolutionary or critical praxis must both critique the resulting ideological explanations and transform those relations which constitute the social contradictions. In so doing, she reveals what Freire means by liberation that moves from the liberal humanist notion of "traditional democratic freedom" to that of freeing oneself and others from the relation of the dialectical contradiction. She understands how, without reading Freire through Marx, his ideas can become perilously domesticated at most, and at the very least rendered imprecise and abstracted from their revolutionary or transformative intent. Marx's negative conception of ideology—to which Freire's work is intimately connected—is not that of a "false consciousness" but refers to actions and symbols that constitute explanations that are really only partial and fragmented and, therefore, distorted.

Freire is clear that education and cultural processes aimed at liberation succeed not by freeing people from their chains but by preparing them collectively to free themselves. This is dialectically facilitated when conversation is replaced by a dialogical praxis. Whereas conversation or discussion focuses on what we think and helps people articulate their interpretation of reality against others (in this regard it resembles a form of "managed communication of monologues"), dialogue, on the other hand, involves the critical investigation of knowledge—not only of what we think, but also why we think as we do. Allman is correct in claiming, along with Freire, that trust does not preexist dialogue but is created within the act of dialogue itself, "*haciendo el camino al andar*" [making the road as we walk].

Revolutionary Social Transformation is a timely and provocative book that could not be better suited for these educational times. It is a book that rescues Freire and Gramsci from their liberal exponents and refunctions them within a Marxian legacy where they first drew breath. The educational left here in North America and elsewhere would do well to make this book an integral part of the education of their students.

Peter McLaren
Los Angeles

REFERENCES

Brenner, Robert (1998). "The Economics of Global Turbulence." *New Left Review, 229*, 1–264.

Hobsbawm, Eric (1998). "The Death of Neo-Liberalism." *Marxism Today* (November–December), 4–8.

Kundnani, Arun (1998/99). "Where Do You Want to Go Today? The Rise of Information Capital." *Race & Class, 40*, No. 2/3, 49–71.

Ollman, Bertell (1998). "Why Dialectics? Why Now?" *Science & Society, 62*, No. 3 (Fall), 338–357.

Acknowledgments

I could not possibly name all of the individuals to whom I am indebted; therefore I will try to be brief.

I sincerely and affectionately thank Margaret and David Warsop for encouraging me to see this project through to completion. I also thank Professor Dick Geary for his encouragement and for helping me to further clarify my thinking about dialectical thinking. I owe many thanks to my friend and colleague, Dr. Peter Mayo, who put me in touch with Henry Giroux and who has supported me and stimulated my thinking in many ways. I also am very grateful to Henry Giroux for his support and to him and Jane Garry for the work and commitment they have put into the publication of this book.

The students who originally encouraged me to apply Paulo Freire's educational approach and the many since who shared this approach to education with me have taught me a great deal and have been a constant source of inspiration. They stimulated my thinking, my reflection and the improvements that were made in the use of Freire's ideas. It was their questions and our dialogues that necessitated a rigorous study of Marx and my analysis of the influence of his ideas on both Freire and Gramsci. There are no words to adequately thank them; nevertheless my gratitude is theirs. In addition I am extremely indebted to my colleague, Dr. John Wallis, who shared this praxis with me and with whom I also have written several articles. He has continually helped me clarify and refine my thinking, as I trust I have his.

Perhaps most importantly I want to thank my wonderful friends/family for their love and support and to give special thanks to my friends Margaret Bauder, Ivan Barker, Jill Vincent, Maggie and David Richmond, Brenda and David Jackson, and Susan and Mary Wallis for their continual help and support. I also want to give special thanks to Margaret Worsop who typed the original manuscript virtually without error, to Mary Wallis and David Richmond for their patience and assistance with matters related to my use of the computer and to Klara and Eric King for all their help with the final stages of this project..

Of course, I am eternally indebted to Marx, Freire and Gramsci for their contributions to my thinking—my praxis. However, to Freire I owe a special debt for helping me to establish a coherence between faith, knowledge and political commitment.

REVOLUTIONARY SOCIAL TRANSFORMATION

1

Introduction: Rationale and Orientation

Social divisions and various forms of injustice are escalating. These tendencies have increased to a pernicious degree over the past three decades, and they penetrate local, regional, national and global levels of human existence. This book is intended to be a contribution to developing an effective collective challenge to this situation, a challenge that will involve social transformation at all these levels of human existence. The human condition is not only riddled with injustice and oppressive divisions, it is illogical. It does not make any rational or ethical sense for these tendencies to be on the increase at a point in history when the human and technological capacity to produce goods and services has never been greater. This capacity has been created within human history, by human beings, and it could be used to meet the needs of *all* human beings while also protecting and sustaining our natural environment. I will be advocating this objective as the major goal of social transformation.

Achieving this goal will depend upon a quite massive and collective human effort. Authentic social transformation is never a sudden event. It is a process through which people change not only their circumstances but themselves. Consequently it must be an educational process that involves the simultaneous transformation of educational relations. Since in the first instance this book addresses those people who engage, or wish to engage, with others to bring about social transformation in various, eventually all, levels of human existence, one theme in particular provides a cohesive thread throughout the chapters. This theme is human consciousness and our need to understand how it is constituted and how it can be rendered more critical. These understandings are the necessary bases for transforming the educational relations and developing forms of engagement that can lead to, and eventually bring about, justice for all humankind.

I explain why I think this understanding of consciousness is so fundamental to achieving authentic social change. My own commitment to the importance of human consciousness has developed from a serious questioning of certain characteristics of the human condition. I have questioned, for example, why so many people throughout human history have accepted the human condition as something inevitable and natural, and why it should be that this acceptance comes from not only those who are comfortable but also those who suffer and who are oppressed within the social relations of their existence. This anomalous situation has taken on an added dimension in our present historical conjuncture.

For a good part of the twentieth century, many people thought they were witnessing the socialist/communist alternative for social-economic societal organization. In my opinion there was too little questioning of whether the practice and experience of this alternative was an accurate expression of the theory or vision of socialism/communism. As a consequence, when the alternative collapsed in many nation states, the death knell of a possible global alternative was sounded. Some people retreated into localized, often atomized or individualized, attempts to better their human condition. Others embraced and championed the further penetration of capitalist social relations throughout the world, together with the highly compromised forms of democratic governance that have developed historically within those relations. Although many of us have remained critical of a great deal of what passed for socialism/communism and also hopeful that this alternative vision can still be realized, we face additional problems in confronting the "myth" of the naturalness and inevitability of the past and present human condition. The illogical "logic" that there is no alternative to capitalism has become increasingly widespread. Nevertheless, this book is intended as a contribution to mounting an effective challenge to that logic. It should be noted that the material reality of capitalism also offers a contribution to this challenge.

My emphasis on the importance of understanding human consciousness is directly related to the process of engaging in this and other challenges. Understanding consciousness and its *inner* connection with human practice provides answers to many of the political, educational and ethical questions we must consider. It also provides ideas for developing a strategy that can challenge ourselves and others to engage in more creative and critical ways of thinking and acting.

It is sometimes difficult to interpret the distinction that some people draw between a practical and a theoretical text. I intend to provide a text that embraces the intimate link between these two, but I anticipate that some readers may consider it to be too theoretical and not practical enough for their purposes. I can only say that the theory or ideas discussed here arose from practice aimed at social transformation for justice and were refined and elaborated through application within those sites of practice just as they must be within the readers' own experiences. They should also help us reflect upon and understand the efforts of others both contemporaneously and historically. Throughout human history, some human beings have critically intervened to challenge and often change what seemed to be the natural and inevitable course of human history, to thwart the forward march of injustice and social division. Social change has been won through struggle, but often these "victories" have involved access to something like political voice, education or the expression of our cultural differences that have already become devalued in terms of their potential to promote social division. In other words, they have become domesticated. Furthermore, certain major "victories" like the establishment of greater and lesser welfare states may well prove to be short-lived in historical terms. There is a fundamental difference between social reform and authentic social transformation. Even when well intended and offering temporary relief for many people, reforms often do not go deep enough to destroy the roots of oppression in a truly radical manner. In fact, the activists engaged in these struggles have often lacked an understanding of those roots and have therefore based their campaigns on access to the "given" rights and privileges of others rather than a critical appraisal and attempt to transform the form of these. Nevertheless, since it is human beings who make history, it follows that we can intervene to change history in an authentically radical way. However, we will need a rigorously critical theory to guide and critique our action, our interventions. This book represents an attempt to provide some of the essential foundations for developing such a theory.

I have implied already that this book is addressed, in the first instance, to radicals, especially those who perceive the educational nature of engaging with others and who understand the importance of their own learning—that is, the mutuality and reciprocity of learning—within these engagements. Obviously such engagements involve political party activists and those involved in various social movements, but they also involve many others with much less explicit roles who share a commitment to social transformation for justice. I also hope to address the many people who, as yet, are only concerned about or uncomfortable with the current human condition as they or others experience it.

A range of critical theory and research, related to economics, politics, globalization and education, underpins the orientation of this book. However, the discussion is based primarily on the analysis, theory and theorization of practice of three people. In order of emphasis they are Karl Marx, Paulo Freire and Antonio Gramsci. Through their original texts (at least those available in English translation), they have assisted me to theorize and creatively develop my own practice, whether it is focused on formal or informal attempts to engage in education for social transformation. Even though this book, itself, is a secondary source and therefore an interpretation, I want to encourage readers to seek out, read and study the original texts. I do not argue my interpretations against those of other secondary-source authors (although I am well aware of many of them), because I want, to the best of my ability, to communicate the ideas of Marx, Freire and Gramsci (and some of my own based on them) directly to the reader. I think that much too often texts are considered by readers as highly theoretical and therefore inaccessible because writers interrupt their conversation with the reader to engage in conversations or debates with other authors.

The original texts of Freire and Gramsci, in comparison to Marx, are fairly accessible. In the case of Marx, I will be drawing on sources that were written over a period of forty years. To increase readers' access to these, I often offer alternative publications when the English translations are compatible. In the text the dates pertaining to Marx's writings follow a convention I found in Derek Sayer (1987) and which I find very useful in developing a historical sense of the development and coherence of Marx's thinking: I use the date at which Marx last worked on a particular piece, according to Sayer. The actual publication dates of the sources appear in the references. Also, to assist readers who wish to engage in further study, I offer page numbers or ranges of page numbers relevant to major ideas even when I have not made a verbatim quote.

I must emphasize that all my discussions of theory and ideas are meant to be contributions to our project for social transformation.

Since social transformation is needed at all levels of human existence, it means that engagement in radical action can begin almost anywhere. It also means that some people can engage with many levels simultaneously. However, all these efforts must be linked and eventually organized as well as cemented by shared visions and values regarding the global human society we are striving to create. Therefore, we need to communicate and begin to openly debate the visions and alternatives that are possible. This book represents an attempt to communicate, to offer visions and alternatives that others will need to debate. Many other texts with a critical perspective offer this sort of basis. But people do not need to depend solely on written communication to inform or trigger their discussions. They can search together for their visions and alternatives that would lead to greater justice for all. Nevertheless, at some point, a coherence and consensus will need to be forged to coordinate and organize all our seemingly disparate efforts. First, however, we need to share not only what we are doing but also our reflections on why we have chosen to engage in a particular struggle and how we think this might relate to the global campaign for social transformation.

Many people become activists with reference to a single issue. Some of these issues emanate from or seem to reside solely in our local contexts. As I think over various issues or problems that have enlisted people in local activism—for example, a village-level struggle for clean water; confrontations with racism/racial violence in a school or neighborhood; gender oppression and harassment at a workplace; access for the socially disabled to public transport in their own city; the fight against age discrimination with reference to a particular job; or a local campaign to prohibit nuclear waste dumping or to prevent a multinational corporation with unsafe work practices and destructive end-products from locating production in a particular area—I find it difficult, if not impossible, to see these as isolated events over local issues and problems. Each of the examples I have cited, and many more, is a global issue, and those engaged in local struggle need to understand the global significance of what they do. When they do not see the link, the result is often that their problem simply is shifted to another place, another community, or victories won are used to defuse and depoliticize—that is, domesticate—the crucial significance of the local effort.

We need to go further than this understanding of the global nature of single issues. We need to develop a critical understanding of how all of these and other issues link together in a total structure, a human structure, of oppression welded together by the social relations and objectives of global capitalism. At least in certain areas of activism that imply such an understanding, or the beginning of it, this is beginning to happen. For example, environmental groups have joined trade unions and worked together in the recent past with antiapartheid activists to demonstrate against and challenge the activities of offending multinationals (Bond, 1990). Women have joined together globally to confront and boycott a multinational that was dispensing "free" dried infant formula to women in areas of the world with no clean water supply. We need more inside information about the internal workings of such efforts, their successes and failures, so that we can learn from them and so that we can create many more unified efforts that can begin from an enhanced base of information and experience. In short, we need to communicate in order to bring the vision and direction of our struggles into sharp focus.

One last point about communication is necessary. Human beings often differentiate themselves from—and as a consequence elevate themselves above—other species due to the human ability to communicate. A further tendency is to subdivide the human species according to what are considered to be greater and lesser abilities to communicate within the parameters of a Eurocentric tradition. The first differentiation has led to insidious uses and abuses of other species and the supposedly rational acceptance of these practices. It also has meant that we have learned little from observing, "listening" to, the ways in which other species do communicate with each other and often try to communicate with us. The second differentiation has led to outright oppression through the suppression of other voices. In this case, we have also failed to listen and learn. Therefore, my stress on communication demands that we strive to improve this ability, to listen and to speak with both our hearts and minds and to empathically and systematically question what both we ourselves and others think. We cannot achieve the visions and alternatives proposed here without improving our, at present, very stunted ability to communicate.

The book is comprised of six chapters that are intended to interlink and form a coherent whole. Chapter 1, you have almost finished. Chapter 2, "The Vision," contains some critique of the human condition and a view of the kind of human relations that we could create. It is a vision of the process of social transformation based on the writings of Karl Marx, the vision to which I am committed. It is primarily an expression of values rather than a blueprint, as the latter would thwart the creative intervention of human beings. This creative intervention is one of the—if not the—most fundamental values in Marx's vision; therefore, a blueprint would be sheer hypocrisy. In no way do I want to suggest that this vision is the only alternative. I am simply saying that this is the basis, the bedrock, of my vision, and am trying to make explicit the vision that underpins the selection of topics and theory discussed in the other chapters. Chapter 3 is about Marx's revolutionary theory of human consciousness, which postulates the *inner* connection between social existence and thought. I explain why this makes it a theory of praxis, and I draw a clear distinction between limited/reproductive praxis and critical/revolutionary (transformative) praxis. To elaborate further on critical consciousness/praxis, I have devoted chapter 4 to a discussion of Marx's dialectical mode of conceptualizing and important aspects of his understanding of capitalist reality. Throughout the book and with the use of examples, I also offer readers an introduction to Marx's critique of capitalist economies—his explanation of capitalism. By explaining the dialectical contradictions of capitalism, and especially their historical development, I also hope to offer an explanation for the fairly recent globalization of capitalist social relations of production and the tendency to commodify increasingly many aspects of our social existence.

In chapter 5, the focus is turned to a consideration of the contributions of Paulo Freire and Antonio Gramsci. Both of these men engaged in the process of social transformation, albeit in different arenas, and both attempted to explicate the theory behind the practice they advocated. I argue that there are many important parallels in their thinking because both base their ideas on an understanding of Marx's theory of consciousness. Even though Marx stressed the importance of prefigurative action and struggle as a means of preparing people to engage in authentic social change, he never discussed, in any detail, the process of preparation. However, this is the major contribution that Freire and Gramsci offer, and it is the basis I use for comparing their ideas.

In the final chapter, I return to vision and offer some initial ideas about re-creating democracy as well as our concepts of equality and truth so that we can begin to face the challenge of authentically transforming our social existence in order to create social and economic justice on a global scale.

REFERENCES

Bond, P. (1990). "The New U.S. Class Struggle: Financial Industry Power vs. Grassroots Populism." *Capital and Class*, No. 40 (Spring), 150–181.

Sayer, D. (1987). *The Violence of Abstraction*. London: Basil Blackwell.

2

The Vision

Without vision, or what can be called social imagination, the type of social transformation advocated in this book would be impossible. If we are going to create a more humanized form of existence, we need at least a broad notion of what this would entail. Any vision worth striving for must be realistic rather than whimsical. It must be based on considerations and critiques of the past and present human condition. In other words, to be achievable, a vision must be derived from the real, the material world.

In this chapter, my vision is made explicit because it is the one that underpins the entire book, and readers should be aware of this. I do not intend to imply that this is the only vision but rather to share with you a possible vision for your consideration. I will give it a label that I use synonymously and interchangeably, throughout the book, with social transformation aimed at humanization. My vision is based on the meaning of socialism/communism which can be culled from the writings of Karl Marx. When I share this meaning with you, I trust that you will see that it has had very little reflection in the most well-known and publicized experiences of twentieth-century "actually existing socialism." There are many valid historical reasons for this failure to integrate theory and practice, but in our own stage of history these reasons, or excuses, should no longer pertain. They have become unviable due to at least two very important factors. We now have access, at least in English translation, to the full range of Marx's writings from which his meaning of socialism/communism must be drawn. We also have a world of global capitalism, with all the consequent forms of inhumanity related to this form of economic organization of human production. However, ironically we also have a productive capacity that, once transformed within humanized forms of social relations, is capable of meeting the needs of all human beings.

Marx's ideas about socialism and communism have inspired my work and my life. I have found no person with a greater or more promising vision of what an authentic creation of "human history" would entail. My account of Marx's "meaning" is culled from his writings over the forty tumultuous years during which he developed and refined his thinking.

I must emphasize that, according to my interpretation, Marx's ideas and analyses were materially based and never utopian, in the worst sense of that word. Nevertheless, when one's pronouncements challenge, so concretely and hopefully, the seemingly inevitable given conditions, they can seem utopian. This applies to his own time, and perhaps to the subsequent adulterations of his thought. It also applies to our own time, when the full realization of the capitalism he critiqued is even more real, immediate and seemingly insurmountable.

I make no claims that overcoming capitalism and other aspects of injustice and oppression will be easier given a clearer vision of what we might be trying to create. However, I cannot understand how we can get anywhere without a clear and realistic vision. This brings me back full circle to the purpose of this chapter. We must begin to debate what we mean by socialism and social transformation. It can do no harm to inform this debate by going back to Marx and perhaps others. I am suggesting that we begin with Marx.

WHY WE NEED SOCIALISM AND WHY WE NEED TO BE CLEAR

At a time when the four horsemen of the apocalypse—nuclear annihilation of life; destruction of the eco-systems and the biosphere; hunger in the Third World; massive impoverishment among the northern hemisphere's victims of the "dual society"—are breathing down our necks . . . socialism or misery and barbarism, with the palpable risk of actual extinction . . . this is the choice before humankind today. [Mandel, 1988, p. 113]

If this is to be a truly human choice, people need to be clear about what they are choosing. Anthony Wright encapsulates the problem:

a century after the socialist revival of the 1880s the "radiant ambiguities of the word socialism" (Tawney's phrase) seemed more radiant then ever. [Wright, 1983, p. 25]

Everything one says about socialism necessarily hinges on the definition of socialism that one is using; therefore, I must begin by making my meaning explicit. In so doing I will be indicating agreement with the comments of Ernest Mandel that socialism is necessary, but I also intend to add to this the argument that it is desirable. However, if humankind is to freely choose socialism, we are going to need far more than a definition. We will need an "approach" to all forms of political engagement which allows people to experience, even if only as a relatively brief encounter, what we are encouraging them to choose. Clearly, to develop an "approach" that reflects the socialist alternative we need an unambiguous concept of what we are trying to achieve. My aim, as I have said, is not to convince you that the meaning proposed here is correct, but to encourage a wider debate, a rethink, so that soon instead of "radiant ambiguities" we can move forward with a clear purpose in mind.

SOCIALISM: THE FOUNDATIONS

As I have stated, the concept of socialism I discuss here is taken entirely from the writings of Karl Marx. To reiterate: the reason for choosing Marx's concept is twofold. Socialism is not going to descend on us from heaven or outer space; it has got to be developed out of our present conditions. For most people in the contemporary world, these are the conditions of capitalism, a historically specific social form. Some of the phenomenal content of these conditions may have changed since the time when Marx wrote and may vary from place to place, but the form, the underlying essence or dialectical contradictions, that Marx exposed remains. Therefore, Marx's idea of the new reality we could develop out of the old seems to provide the most realistic way forward.

However, Marx was not only capitalism's severest and most accurate critic; he was also one of humanity's greatest moral philosophers. His concept of socialism is both scientific (dialectical) and ethical.

Marx had a vision of what human beings could become. It was, however, a vision based not on a mere faith in humanity but rather on a materialist analysis of the human condition. That analysis began before, but always motivated, his detailed analysis of the reasons for the conditions—the same conditions that we continue to endure, even if for some people enduring takes the form of wealth and comfort. I hope it is clear that I prefer Marx's concept of socialism because it is based on real possibilities rather than utopian dreams. Unfortunately, our daily experience within capitalist societies so blinds us to these possibilities that when we do express them they may sound utopian. This is one reason why we need political action for socialism, which starts with that experience and which helps us remove the blind spots. It seems to follow that all such action will have to contain the type of educational encounter advocated by Freire (1972) and Gramsci (1971). I discuss their ideas later in the book because both Freire and Gramsci emphasize the important if not central role of education within any form of political or cultural action for socialism. Both of them base their ideas on Marx's materialist theory of consciousness (e.g. Marx and Engels, 1846). They recognize that all people are conscious beings; therefore, education is not about the didactic "filling-up" of empty minds with knowledge but of enabling people's already existing activity of thinking to become a critical and critically conscious activity.

Marx's concept of socialism can only be grasped if we consider what he said about both socialism and communism. He preferred the latter term but often used socialism interchangeably with it. He invented neither term. In fact his own idea of either socialism or communism was usually revealed in his critiques of other people's ideas about socialism and what he called "crude communism" (Marx, 1844b, p. 88). If we are going to cull his meaning, therefore, we cannot let the terminology get in our way, even if many readers hold quite different or even opposing ideas about these two forms of political and economic organization. Marx, however, did offer a way in which we might begin to distinguish between socialism and communism. This is the distinction that has been adopted within, at least the rhetoric of, many revolutionary movements. Marx talked about two different phases of communism. The first phase would still contain some of the defects of capitalism.

> But these defects are inevitable in the first phase of communist society as it is when it has just emerged after the prolonged birth pangs from capitalist society. [Marx, 1875, p. 569]

The first phase was to entail the eradication of those defects and the preparation for a second, fully communist phase—a classless, non-antagonistic social formation (Marx and Engels, 1848, pp. 236–238). I prefer to keep the distinction and the relationship between the two phases in view by referring to the first as socialism and the second as communism. Socialism is therefore the process of creating a new social formation by abolishing the defects of the previous one. To understand that process or the first phase, we also have to understand the second. These phases are not only distinguishable but also intimately related. This is because to achieve the second phase in an authentic way will necessitate a change in human consciousness. According to Marx's theory of consciousness (see aspects below), changes in consciousness are predicated on changes in social relations, our social being.

When Marx and Engels first wrote about their materialist conception of history they clearly depicted the first phase as a process or movement:

> Communism is for us not a state of affairs which is to be established, an ideal to which reality will have to adjust itself. We call communism the real movement which abolishes the present state of things. The conditions of this movement result from the premisses now in existence. [Marx and Engels, 1846, p. 171][1]

And more precisely later in the same piece, they say:

> Communism differs from all previous movements in that it overturns the basis of all earlier relations of production and intercourse and for the first time consciously treats all natural premisses as the creatures of hitherto existing men, strips them of their natural character and subjugates them to the power of the united individuals. [p. 179][2]

In other words, this was the movement of the "united individuals," a movement that could only succeed when people recognized that there was nothing natural or inevitable about existing relations. These were produced by human beings, the products of their history. To "consciously treat" the existing premises as the result of history meant a change in thinking. So the first phase of communism involved people learning to think critically about their existence and recognizing that there was no reason for people to be dominated by circumstances. The "united individuals" could begin to actively create their own history rather than simply participating in the creation of their own domination. The movement was about creating a new reality, but because "for the first time" this involved human beings consciously engaged in actively producing that reality, that history, it was also the beginning of it (Marx and Engels, 1846, pp. 159–191).

Since the second phase was to be the creation of the "united individuals," Marx's proposals were primarily about what should be abolished. He therefore offered no precise blueprint for communism, only some very general principles that followed directly from his critique of the existing "relations of production and intercourse."

A BRIEF EXPLORATION OF MARX'S CRITIQUE OF CAPITALISM AND THE "SOCIALIST" RESPONSE TO ITS DEFECTS

In the passage cited above (Marx and Engels, 1846, p. 179), Marx is saying that the main defects of capitalism, and all previous social formations, can be attributed to the relations of production and intercourse. At different points in history the relations of capitalism produce different problems or defects, such as some of the relatively recent ones that the Mandel quote detailed earlier in this chapter. However, there are also more essential defects—in fact, dialectical contradictions—which constitute the general character of capitalism throughout its development. It is these we must consider to get at Marx's concept of the socialist/communist alternative. Abolishing these would create the possibility for abolishing those about which Mandel spoke and many others.

In common with previous social formations, capitalism involves the exploitation of one class by another. One class actually produces the material wealth of the society, but another commands the results of that production. Those who command the results also decide what is to be produced, whether it be pyramids or nuclear weapons. However, in each distinctive social formation there are historically specific differences in the economic relations within which this exploitation takes place (Marx, 1858, pp. 83–99).[3] For all class-divided societies, the productive class has to produce a surplus beyond what is necessary to the continuing existence of that class. If they did not, there would be nothing for the exploiters. In previous social formations it was obvious that one class produced a surplus product that another class enjoyed, and a way of thinking about these relations had to be developed so that people would accept them as natural and inevitable (pp. 156–158).[4] Under capitalism, one class continues to create a surplus that makes the existence of another class possible, but this is far from obvious—so far from obvious that many people think just the reverse, viz. that it is the exploiting class, the capitalists, that creates the material world and its own wealth (p. 321).[5] Marx first set out a materialist concept of history so that people could understand that they not only produce their material world but in so doing they produce themselves (Marx and Engels, 1846). He then went on to analyze dialectically the actual relations that enable the capitalists to extract a surplus value out of the wage labor they employ (Marx, 1858; also the four volumes of *Capital*: 1863, 1865, 1867, 1878).[6] However, to actually understand that major defect of capitalism, a defect it shares with all previous social forms, one has to develop a materialist concept of history and the role that people, so far, have played in it. Marx, together with Engels, explained what this concept entails:

> The premisses from which we begin are not arbitrary ones, not dogmas, but real premisses from which abstractions can only be made in the imagination. They are the real individuals, their activity and the material conditions under which they live, both those they find already existing and those produced by their activity. . . . [People] can be distinguished from animals by consciousness. . . . They themselves begin to distinguish themselves from animals as soon as they begin to produce their means of subsistence, a step which is conditioned by their physical organisation. . . . The way in which [people] produce the means of subsistence depends first of all on the nature of the actual means of subsistence they find in existence and have to reproduce. This mode of production must not to be considered simply as being the production of physical existence. . . . Rather it is a definite form of activity of these individuals, a definite form of expressing their life. . . . As individuals express their life, so they are. What they are, therefore, coincides with their production, both with *what* they produce and *how* they produce. The nature of individuals thus depends on the material conditions determining their production. [Marx and Engels, 1846, pp. 160–161][7]

Material conditions include the economic relations. If these allow one class to extract a surplus from another and yet people either accept this as natural or do not recognize it (i.e. do not "treat it consciously"), then what we are as human beings is severely limited (Marx, 1844b).[8] We cannot distinguish human beings from animals by virtue of consciousness if their consciousness accepts the given state of affairs as natural and inevitable, thus enabling them to collude in producing either their own or other people's exploitation. Material comforts have nothing to do with eliminating the problem, the defect—although, of course, when wages rise it makes the lives of working-class people far more bearable. Marx was very concerned about the degree of financial impoverishment that the working class was suffering during his lifetime, and he foresaw that capitalism would create growing numbers of unemployed—the underclass that is one of the most heinous results of our contemporary world (Marx, 1867, p. 483).[9] But he also was concerned about another form of impoverishment. He felt that if people were not "treating" their world consciously (i.e. critically), then they were not fulfilling their potential as human beings. Their humanity was impoverished because their consciousness was uncritical (Marx, 1844b). This was a consciousness that served the purpose of reproducing the social relations of oppression, even frequently when it was directed at resistance to the given state of affairs.

Marx's idea of what human beings could be was not some whim of his imagination. His vision of this potential was derived from a historical and material analysis of the real world. All human beings were part of the same biological species, and one of the characteristics of that species is conscious thought. According to Marx, it was unreasonable to think that those who had the power to make decisions and to direct the course of history were somehow inherently superior—a species apart from the rest. Instead, it was the antagonistic class relations that constrained "the free," the critical, consciousness of the majority. But even the minority's consciousness was not "free" (Marx and Engels, 1845); money was the "logic of their minds" (Marx, 1844b, pp. 99, 109–111).[10] Marx reasoned that if we are a species characterized by consciousness, then all people must be consciously engaged in their own self-determination. As we express our lives, so we are.

Marx, therefore, tried to provide us with a way of understanding our reality which would enable us to develop the consciousness we would need for abolishing the current defects and creating a new reality. Although he acknowledged that it was not easy, he thought that we could learn to grasp the actual relations that produce definite material results (Marx, 1865, p. 956).[11] Some of these results were progressive, or rather would be if they were used to benefit all of humankind. For example, the relations of capitalism have led to the development of massive productive forces—greater now even than in Marx's time. These could be harnessed to meeting humanity's needs and in alliance with the needs of the environment. Instead, however, under capitalism the productive forces are used to generate profit and the accumulation and concentration of capital. This leads, among other things, to the creation of recurring crises of "overproduction" (pp. 289–301, 358–367).[12] Not overproduction in terms of what the people of the world need, of course, but in capitalist terms.

In these crises, a spate of commodities is produced. These are of no use to their owners because they cannot be sold. Not enough people want them or are able to buy them. Demand or need, as readers know, has to do with purchasing power. When supply exceeds that sort of demand, the only solution to the crisis is to destroy what has been produced or create "mountains" of the surplus. In addition, when crises are severe even some of the existing forces of production—plant and machinery—are destroyed. Some capitalists and their capital are sacrificed so that others can survive. Marx thought that this was blatantly ridiculous (Marx, 1865). He was scathing in his criticism and would have been more so had he understood what we know today, viz. that this "overproduction" is also contributing to the destruction of valuable, irreplaceable natural resources and with them the world's ecosystems and biosphere.[13]

Marx's analysis of capitalism is an analysis of how specific relations produce specific results. One of these results was capital itself. If you destroyed the relation that produced capital, you would no longer have capital or capitalism (Marx and Engels, 1845, pp. 49–54).[14] In other words, according to Marx we cannot reform capitalism. It can be made temporarily more palatable, but so long as capitalist relations exist, the deplorable mess they create will continue to emerge on an ever-wider scale. In Marx's time, the critics of capitalism tended to perceive the results as the real problem rather than their relational source. This led to the idea that the defects could be reformed.[15] Contemporary critics still entertain some of the same reformist ideas that Marx criticized his contemporary socialists for advocating. For example, we focus on the unfair distribution of resources and the contrast between the very rich and the very poor and come up with solutions like taxing the rich so that some of their wealth can be redistributed to the poor. Or we think that if we transfer the means of production from private to public or cooperative ownership, then workers will no longer be exploited. Marx agreed that private ownership and distribution were real problems, but he saw them as the defective results of the capitalist relations of production and intercourse. He thought that he had made it clear that if you don't change the relations, the inherent contradictions of capitalism, in the long term you change nothing. Understandably, therefore, we can hear his frustration in his reply to the German Social Democratic Workers Party's Gotha programme:

> it was in general a mistake to make a fuss about so-called distribution and put the principal stress on it. Any distribution whatever of the means of consumption is only a consequence of the distribution of the conditions of production themselves. The latter distribution, however, is a feature of the mode of production itself. The capitalist mode of production, for example, rests on the fact that the material conditions of production are in the hands of non-workers in the form of property in capital and land, while the masses are only owners of the personal conditions of production, of labour power. If the elements of production are so distributed, then the present-day distribution of the means of consumption results automatically. . . . Vulgar socialism . . . has taken over from the bourgeois economists the consideration and treatment of distribution as independent of the mode of production and hence the presentation of socialism as turning principally on distribution. After the real relation has long been made clear, why retrogress again? [Marx, 1875, pp. 569–570]

Of course, the idea of a "free association of producers" owning the means of production was central to Marx's idea of socialism, but he was assuming that with that ownership the whole *raison d'être* for production would change. It would be production for human need rather than for profit. Only by changing the goal of production would the real exploitation of labor cease (pp. 568–569).[16] We should have understood this point by now because Britain and some other capitalist countries have had the actual experience of public and cooperative ownership of some of the means of production. As long as those industries must compete within capitalist markets, they must play the capitalist game, and the relations of exploitation remain.

Furthermore, to focus on ownership alone is to focus on something that has become a result of the labor–capital relation. That statement needs further explanation because it relates to one of the most complex concepts to arise from Marx's analysis. When Marx set out the entire historical development of capitalism, he showed how certain preconditions made possible the historically specific relations of capitalism. They actually predated the relations. One of these preconditions was an accumulation of wealth that made the ownership of the means of production possible. However once the specific labor–capital relation had developed, then all further ownership of the means of production, the possibility of capital accumulation, derives from the relation. Therefore what began as a precondition or cause becomes a result, but a result that can only be eliminated when the relation between labor and capital is abolished, if we are to produce revolutionary change (Marx, 1858, pp. 502–514).[17]

Throughout Marx's critiques of "crude communism" and socialist thought, he was actually criticizing a way of thinking that has important implications for socialist strategy. He criticized the French socialist, Proudhon, for thinking that the major problem was money. He argued that getting rid of money while retaining capitalist commodity production was akin to getting rid of catholicism while retaining the Pope (Marx, 1867, p. 181 fn.). And even though Marx himself was an atheist, he urged other socialists to focus their critique on earth rather than heaven. It is important to look at the full passage, since it is often quoted in an abbreviated way that serves to distort his meaning:

> Religious suffering is at the same time an expression of real suffering and a protest against real suffering. Religion is the sigh of the oppressed creature, the feeling of a heartless world, and the soul of soulless circumstances. It is the opium of the people. The abolition of religion as the illusory happiness of the people is the demand for their real happiness. The demand to give up the illusions about their condition is a demand to give up a condition that requires illusion. The criticism of religion is therefore the form of the criticism of the valley of tears whose halo is religion. Criticism has plucked the imaginary flowers from the chains not so that man may bear chains without any imagination or comfort, but so that he may throw away the chains and pluck living flowers. The criticism of religion disillusions man so that he may think, act and fashion his own reality as a disillusioned man come to his senses; so that he may revolve around himself as his real sun. Religion is only the illusory sun which revolves around man as long as he does not revolve around himself. It is, therefore, the task of history, now the truth is no longer in the beyond, to establish the truth of the here and now.

> The first task of philosophy, which is in the service of history, once the holy form of human self-alienation has been discovered, is to discover self-alienation in its unholy forms. The criticism of heaven is thus transformed into the criticism of earth, the criticism of religion into the criticism of law, and the criticism of theology into the criticism of politics. [Marx, 1844c, p. 64][18]

Over and over again in his writings, Marx was trying to help us grasp the real relations, the causes of the problems. Only when we transform these can we begin to *change the world* (Marx, 1845, "Theses on Feuerbach," No. XI).

Therefore, Marx's concept of socialism was of a struggle to abolish all the antagonistic relations that make capitalism possible. Of course, economic relations are central, and were Marx's main focus, but these relations also condition many others, whether they are those between different races, genders, ages or whatever. However, since capitalist economic relations only condition these other relations, we cannot assume that abolishing capitalist production and exchange relations will automatically eliminate the antagonisms in these other areas. The origins of these other relations do not lie solely in capitalist history. It is only that, under capitalism, they take on one particular form rather than another (Marx, 1858, pp. 483–514).[19] Therefore political action for socialism and socialism itself must involve us in struggling to change relations in every aspect of our daily experience. It is through this struggle and the changed relations that we also will begin to transform ourselves and prepare ourselves to create and live in a new reality. As I mentioned before, Marx left no precise blueprint for a communist society, and to expect him to have done so would be to misunderstand his whole project. However, he did suggest some guidelines or principles about certain features of life under the two phases of communism which we should consider.

SOCIALISM: HISTORICAL STRUGGLE ALLOWS MARX TO ELABORATE ON THE FOUNDATIONS

In the preface to the second German edition of the *Communist Manifesto,* Marx corrected one of the ideas conveyed in the original. This was the idea that the "dictatorship of the proletariat" would involve seizing the apparatuses of the bourgeois state. Although he was not disavowing the principles set out in the original 1848 Manifesto, he was saying they needed to be reworked to fit the specific historical context in which they were to be applied (Marx, 1872, p. 559). It was then 1872 not 1848. Marx had long been a critic of the bourgeois state because it created a separation between political life and other experiences of life. This separation meant that the majority of people gave over their political power to others and therefore were deprived of any meaningful political practice, whether it be decision-making or the execution of decisions (Marx, 1843a).

In his later life, Marx was quite struck by the experience of the Paris Commune wherein the workers had created an alternative political organization and had held power for two months. According to Marx, the only reason why they were defeated in the end was that they failed to take action against enemies both inside and outside the Commune. At any rate, it was the political organization of the Commune that convinced him that the proletariat had a real alternative way of instituting socialism other than through taking over the bourgeois state.

> One thing especially was proved by the Commune, viz. that "the working class cannot simply lay hold of the ready-made state machinery and wield power for its own purposes." [Marx, 1872, p. 559]

Although Marx was well aware that the majority of the Paris Commune was not socialist (Marx, 1881, p. 594), he thought that they had created a form of political organization that would be appropriate for socialism. This is how he described it:

> The Commune—the re-absorption of the state power by society as its own living force instead of as a force controlling and subduing it, by the popular masses themselves, forming their own force instead of the organised force of their suppression—the political form of their own emancipation. [Marx, 1871, p. 555]

Marx goes on to elaborate on what these Parisians had done. They had displaced the army by a National Guard, their own militia, which had the function of defending the people from the government rather than defending the government from the people. The people elected officials who were subject to immediate recall and who were paid the same amount as any other worker. These officials made political decisions in consultation with the people, and they were also responsible for executing the decisions. Politics had become just another type of work within civil society. Marx anticipated that if communes could be developed in every urban area of a state, they could become the organizational vehicle for establishing socialism (Marx, 1871, pp. 555 ff.).

For Marx the Commune's organization would figure in the early period of the first phase of communism. It was primarily about taking the first steps toward abolishing the separation between politics and the majority of people's lived experience within civil society. This "political emancipation" could then pave the way for economic emancipation—the dissolution of the labor–capital relation and the capitalist relations of intercourse (pp. 555 ff.; also Marx, 1843a, pp. 39 ff.).

Economic emancipation would in turn create the conditions for further political emancipation which would involve all people, not just officials, in the "re-absorption" of political power—that is, becoming active in and responsible for the creation and continual re-creation of their society. However, for this to happen the "free association of producers" would have to abolish the economic relations and replace production-for-profit with production-for-need. They also would have to reallocate work so that all the able members of society worked in order to produce things that would satisfy human needs (Marx, 1875).[20] If this were the case and the productive forces were sufficiently developed, then everyone would work for fewer hours. Thus the time would be available for everyone to engage in political discussion, choice and action as well as in a range of other activities, which Marx thought would lead to the all-rounded development of individuals (Marx, 1844b, p. 89).[21]

Marx thought that, under capitalism, individual development was one-sided or narrow and fragmented. With communism, distinctions between work and leisure would be increasingly eroded. There would be a huge diversity of human activity, and all people would freely partake in a range of these. At least this was Marx's concept in his earlier writings where he spoke of the realm of necessity giving way to the realm of freedom (Marx, 1844b). Later he qualified this point because he thought that there would always be some necessary monotonous work that would have to be done to meet human needs. However, if this work were equally distributed among everyone, then no one would have much of it to do, and we could devote most of our time to socially useful, creative work. Marx explains:

> The real wealth of society and the possibility of a constant expansion of its reproduction process does not depend on the length of surplus labour but rather on its productivity and on more or less plentiful conditions of production in which it is performed. The realm of freedom really begins only where labour determined by necessity . . . ends. . . . Just as the savage must wrestle with nature to satisfy his needs to maintain and reproduce his life, so must civilised man, and he must do so in all forms of society and under all possible modes of production. This realm of natural necessity expands with his development, because his needs do too; but the production forces to satisfy these expand at the same time. Freedom, in the sphere [of necessary production], can consist only in this, that . . . the associated producers, govern the human metabolism with nature in a rational way, bringing it under their collective control instead of being dominated by it as a blind power; accomplishing it with the least expenditure of energy and in conditions most worthy and appropriate for their human nature. But this always remains a realm of necessity. The true realm of freedom, the development of human powers [potentials] as an end in itself, begins beyond it, though it can only flourish with the realm of necessity as its basis. [Marx, 1865, pp. 958–959]

In fact, Marx's original assertion that the realm of necessity would give way to a realm of freedom has more to do with our own reality than it did with his. Even though he thought machines would be able to take the place of a great deal of human labor (Marx, 1858, pp. 609, 693 ff., 739), he could not have foreseen the development of the microchip and the possibility that, with socialism, dull, monotonous manufacturing and agricultural work could become the preserve of microchip-driven robots. Nevertheless, he did foresee that life would become increasingly fragmented and meaningless under capitalism, and he urged us to see that there was an alternative.

Marx summed up the second phase of communism in the expression "from each according to his [her] ability to each according to his [her] needs" (Marx, 1875, p. 569). However, for this to become a reality human beings would have to transform their relations in such a way that they actually transformed themselves. We would have to exist as truly social beings who recognized our own individual fulfilment, the expression of our individuality, in fulfilling the needs of others. However, first we would have to understand that our most central need is other human beings. It was in Marx's early writings that he described these transformations most movingly, but it was a vision he never lost. First, he depicts the existing state of affairs:

Our mutual value is for us the value of our mutual products. Thus man himself is for us mutually worthless. [Marx, 1844a, p. 121]

Then he proposes the alternative:

Supposing we had produced in a human manner, each of us would in [our] production have doubly affirmed [ourselves] and [our] fellow [human beings]. I would have: (1) objectified in my production my individuality and its peculiarity and thus both in my activity enjoyed the individual expression of my life and also in looking at the object have had the individual pleasure of realizing that my personality was objective, visible to the senses, and thus a power raised beyond doubt. (2) In your enjoyment or use of my product I would have had the direct enjoyment of realizing that I had both satisfied a human need by my work and also objectified the human essence and therefore fashioned for another human being the object that met his [her] need. (3) I would have been for you the mediator between you and the species and thus been acknowledged and felt by you as a completion of your own essence and a necessary part of yourself and have thus realized that I am confirmed both in your thought and in your love. (4) In my expression of my life I would have fashioned your expression of your life, and thus in my own activity have realized my own essence, my human, my communal essence.

In that case our products would be like so many mirrors, out of which our essence shone.

Thus, in this relationship what occurred on my side would also occur on yours. [pp. 121–122]

Many contemporary marxists would dismiss this passage. They would say that it is the product of the early sentimental, humanist Marx and that it has little to do with the Marx who later produced a rigorous, scientific analysis of capitalism. Nevertheless, many of them would accept the definition or aim of communism quoted earlier, viz. "from each according to his [her] ability to each according to his [her] needs," which was penned eight years before Marx's death and eight years after he had published Volume 1 of *Capital*. It is beyond comprehension how we could arrive at a communist reality, other than by force, without transforming our relations to one another and our perceptions of one another as expressed in the passage above. Perhaps some of the history of the twentieth century gives witness to this point. But, of course, it is only through an authentic praxis of socialism itself that we could fully effect these transformations. I would argue that the difference between the early sentiment and the mature definition was that Marx had worked out precisely what relations would have to be abolished before these transformations could take place. Only with the abolition of existing relations could we begin to realize our species' potential, first and foremost, to need one another and therefore to desire to work reciprocally to meet one another's needs.

Marx's most important guidelines for how socialism can provide a transition to communist relations of production were detailed in the critical comments that he sent to the German socialist Wilhelm Liebknecht. These were written in 1875. He began with a critique of the German socialists' Gotha Programme (the general outline of that critique was covered earlier in this chapter). These socialists were focusing on results rather than on relations or the dialectical contradictions of capitalism; therefore, these were similar criticisms to those he had been making for years. However, these comments also contain his clearest statement of the difference between the two phases of communism or, in my terms, the difference between socialism and communism. He reminded Liebknecht:

> What we have to deal with here is a communist society, not as it has developed on its own foundations but, on the contrary, just as it emerges from capitalist society which is thus, in every respect, economically, morally and intellectually still stamped with the birthmark of the old society from whose womb it emerges. [Marx, 1875, p. 568]

In this letter Marx also argued that the exchange between labor and capital defies the principle of commodity exchange that exchanges should be equal. In the first phase of communism this principle would be reinstated:

> Accordingly, the individual producer receives back from society—after deductions have been made [for the common fund]—exactly what he [she] gives to it. . . . Here obviously the same principle prevails as that which regulates the exchange of commodities, as far as this is exchange of equal values. Content and form are changed because under altered circumstances, no one can give anything but his [her] labour, and because, on the other hand, nothing can pass to the ownership of individuals except individual means of consumption . . . as far as the distribution . . . is concerned . . . a given amount of labour in one form is exchanged for an equal amount of labour in another form [another commodity]. [p. 568]

Therefore, there would be ownership of the commodities that people needed for their individual consumption, but there would be no individual ownership of the means of production. Everyone would produce, and those who genuinely could not would draw from the common fund. In this phase the process simply corrects bourgeois practice, so that the bourgeois principle of equal right is no longer at loggerheads with it. However, this is not enough because, according to Marx, the bourgeois principle of equal right is flawed:

> The right of the producers is proportional to the labour they supply; the equality consists in the fact that the measurement is made with an equal standard, labour.
>
> But one [person] is superior to another physically or mentally and so supplies more labour in the same time, or can labour for a longer time; and labour to serve as a measure must be defined by its duration or intensity, otherwise it ceases to be a standard of measurement. This equal right is an unequal right for unequal labour. It recognises no class differences because everyone is only a worker like everyone else; but it tacitly recognises unequal individual endowment and thus productive capacity as natural privileges. It is, therefore, a right of inequality, in its content, like every right. [pp. 568–569]

According to Marx bourgeois rights are formal or abstract and only exist because real inequalities, based on differences between people, also exist and must be concealed. Under communism, differences between people would not be the basis for oppressive divisions, but rather a source of appreciation because of what they could contribute to the community. He continues:

> Right by its very nature can consist only in the application of an equal standard; but unequal individuals (and they would not be different individuals if they were not unequal) are measurable only by an equal standard in so far as they are brought under an equal point of view, are taken from one definite side only, for instance, in the present case, are regarded only as workers and nothing more is seen in them, everything else being ignored. Furthermore, one worker is married, another not; one has more children than another, and so on. . . . Thus, with an equal performance of labour, and hence an equal share in the social consumption fund, one will in fact receive more than the other, one will be richer than another and so on. To avoid all these defects, right instead of being equal would have to be unequal. [p. 569]

Therefore, it is unequal right that is the basis of a fully developed communist reality—a reality based on the principle: "from each according to his [her] ability, to each according to his [her] needs!" (p. 569). However, a great deal of cultural transformation would have to take place before people would willingly consent to this principle. Marx mentions just a few of these transformations:

> after the enslaving subordination to the division of labour, and therewith also the antithesis between mental and physical labour, has vanished; after labour has become not only a means of life but life's prime want; after the production forces have increased with the all-round development of the individual, and all the springs of co-operative wealth flow more abundantly—only then. [p. 569]

We all could add numerous other transformations that would need to take place, but the real point is that any, or all, of these would be consciously designed by human beings and would be aimed at enabling us to realize that our most fundamental need is one another. Only then would we want to work and produce as much as each of us is capable of doing in order to meet our own needs and the needs of others. In the past and present, the vast majority of people have been compelled to work by force or economic necessity; the choice has never been their own. Marx's idea of communism was of a reality wherein the only form of compulsion was an inner choice, a freely made decision, to meet each other's needs. In other words, we do not require market forces or powerful people to determine the fortunes of some and the misfortunes of others. People can consciously and collectively engage in determining or creating a society of "co-operative wealth" capable of meeting both material and nonmaterial needs.

THE POSSIBILITY OF ACHIEVING MARX'S VISION IN "OUR TIMES"

These, then, were the broad guidelines that Marx proposed. Other points seem to follow. Commodities or products that have a use-value that only becomes available to those who can pay the price of their exchange-value would vanish, as would market exchange. Some form of market or property might remain, but clearly they could not be the forms that arise from capitalist social relations. Of course, we would continue to produce, but only that which people had democratically decided they needed. This could in fact increase real consumer choice of what is actually available rather than leaving the determination to the whims of profitability, competition or government bureaucracies (Mandel, 1988, pp. 115–120). And in comparison to Marx's time, all the decentralized democratic planning and decision-making would be greatly facilitated by advanced information technology.

It also should be noted that Marx's critique of the bourgeois concept of equality moves us in different directions from the present postmodern theorization and practice of recognizing and celebrating difference. Marx does not just recognize or acknowledge differences. He celebrates them by embracing and including the richness that these differences can contribute to establishing a truly human community in local contexts and eventually on a global scale.

Production could be directly aligned to real demand—in other words, need. It also follows that the full realization of Marx's vision would depend on the abolition of capitalism worldwide. Unless, of course, a society is fortunate enough to be totally self-sufficient in meeting its demand for raw materials and natural resources, it is forced to compete in the capitalist world market and therefore to continue some degree of exploitation.

This chapter began with a quote from an article by Ernest Mandel which suggested that there was a worldwide necessity for an alternative international economic order. He proposes socialism. Marx also argued for socialism, pointing to the waste of human life and productive capacity which was the result of the crises inherent to capitalism and market economies. However, I have also tried to indicate that he thought that there was a moral or ethical issue at stake, an issue about what it means to be human. Too often socialists either forget the human issue when they put forward their arguments for socialism or they argue solely on moral grounds. Perhaps this is why, when we mention socialism, so many people immediately picture the color grey or associate it with the idea of "leveling down". Even the most cursory reading of Marx—for example, *The Communist Manifesto* (Marx and Engels, 1848, pp. 233, 243–244)—should have eliminated the idea of "leveling down", yet that idea persists. There are many reasons, but none that can be attributed to Marx.[22] One, surely, is our own failure to grasp the relationship between his vision of humanity and the economic revolution he proposed, together with all the other transformed relations it would entail. If we had grasped this relation, we would already have begun to do far more than talk about socialism. Surely we would have attempted to organize our struggles and to relate to one another in ways that actually reflected the revolutionary option.

For example, formal education, particularly in the postcompulsory sector, could be one aspect of the total struggle for socialism. It is one aspect of our existence where we could begin to challenge bourgeois relations by creating new relations that actually portray an alternative way of existing and knowing. Political work is another extremely important arena. Literally any area of our lives is a possible beginning so long as we have the agreement of others to engage in a struggle for transformation. Marx stressed trade union struggles that could lead on to political struggles as a means by which working people could begin to change themselves, to prepare themselves for socialism (Marx, 1869, p. 538). He says little about education, but it is clear that he thought that it was important and that struggle must be educational. His economic analysis of capitalism was written for working people, and in the late nineteenth and early twentieth centuries many of them read it and formed groups to discuss and study it. However, as truncated texts and dogmatic pamphlets became available, that type of rigorous working-class self-education was eventually eroded (Simon, 1965). I suspect, perhaps because it was once true of myself, that few socialist political activists or other cultural workers of our own time have ever bothered to read what Marx actually said. My aim here has been a simple one: I wanted to whet the socialist appetite for a return to Marx so that together we can begin to clarify what we mean by socialism. I think that Marx's ideas can contribute a great deal to this discussion as well as to our strategies for achieving that particular goal. Apropos of my beginning section, this chapter ends with Mandel:

> If we don't solve that problem first—i.e. the problem of the *goal* of socialists' endeavours—we find ourselves in the unfortunate situation of Louis XVIII's restoration minister, the Duke of Richelieu, who didn't know where he was going [and I must add why] but was absolutely adamant he would arrive there. [Mandel, 1988, p. 108]

NOTES

1. Alternative source: K. Marx and F. Engels, *The German Ideology*, 1846 (Moscow: Progress Publishers, 1976), p. 57.

2. Alternative source: *The German Ideology*, p. 89.

3. Complementary reading: K. Marx, *Capital*, Vol. 1, 1867 (Harmondsworth: Penguin, 1976), p. 325, where Marx says: "What distinguishes the various economic formations of society—the distinction between, for example, a society based on slave-labor and a society based on wage-labor—is the form in which this surplus labor is in each case extorted from the immediate producer, the worker."

4. Complementary reading: *The German Ideology*, pp. 32–102.

5. Complementary reading: *Capital*, Vol. 1, p. 251.

6. He first expressed this in the *Grundrisse*, 1858 (Harmondsworth: Penguin, 1973), but later went into further detail in the four volumes of *Capital*. When I refer to the four volumes of *Capital*, I would emphasize that in addition to the more well-known Volumes 1–3 of *Capital* I am including the three-part work *The Theories of Surplus Value*, 1863 (London: Lawrence & Wishart, Part I, 1967; Part II, 1969; Part III, 1972).

7. Alternative source: *The German Ideology*, pp. 36–37. Throughout the book, brackets within a quotation always indicate that these are my elaborations, alterations or summary comments.

8. Alternative source: *Karl Marx and Frederick Engels Collected Works* [hereafter *MECW*], Vol. 3, 1843–44 (London: Lawrence Wishhart, 1975).

9. Complementary reading: See also chapters 10, 15 and 25 in *Capital*, Vol. 1.

10. Alternative source: *MECW*, Vol. 3, pp. 325–330.

11. It is worth quoting Marx here: "all science [this is the term Marx often used to refer to dialectical conceptualization] would be superfluous if the form of appearance of things directly coincided with their essence [the relations that make the appearances possible]."

12. Pages 289–301 of *Capital*, Vol. 3 (Harmondsworth: Penguin, 1981), offer background explanation, and pp. 358–367 offer an explanation of the overproduction of capital. Complementary reading: *Grundrisse*, pp. 410–423.

13. In fact, Marx understood far more about the effects of capitalist production on the environment than he is often given credit for. On p. 410 of the *Grundrisse*, for example, in a rather complicated passage where he is analyzing the contradictory nature of capital—its tendency to civilize and exploit as part of the same process—he says: "For the first time, nature becomes purely an object of humankind, purely a matter of utility; ceases to be recognized as a power for itself; and the theoretical discovery of its autonomous laws appears merely as a ruse so as to subjugate it under human needs, whether as an object of consumption or a means of production . . . [and with its revolutionizing effects also] the exploitation and exchange of natural and mental forces."

14. Complementary readings: *Grundrisse*, pp. 483–504 (for background regarding property in general); *Capital*, Vol. 1, pp. 1060–1065; *The Poverty of Philosophy*, 1847 (New York: International Publishers, 1969), pp. 186 ff.

15. Complementary readings: Some of the best of these criticisms are in *The Holy Family*, 1845 (London: Lawrence & Wishart, 1956); *The Poverty of Philosophy; The Communist Manifesto*, 1848, in D. McLellan (Ed.), *Karl Marx: Selected Writings* (Oxford: Oxford University Press, 1977), pp. 221–247; *The German Ideology*; *The Theories of Surplus Value*; "The Critique of the Gotha Programme," in McLellan, *Selected Writings* (pp. 564–570).

16. Complementary reading: *Capital*, Vol. 3, pp. 958–959.
17. Complementary reading: *Capital*, Vol. 1, pp. 270–280, 873–876, 1060–1065.
18. It is important to remember that in Marx's time opium was used as a common painkiller.
19. Marx does not discuss these relations explicitly, but inferences can be drawn from several sources: e.g. *Grundrisse*, pp. 483–514; *Economic and Philosophical Manuscripts*, pp. 87–88 in McLellan, *Selected Writings* (on gender relations in particular).
20. Complementary reading: A general theme in the *Grundrisse* and in Volumes 1 and 3 of *Capital*.
21. Complementary reading: *Capital*, Vol. 3, pp. 958–959; "The Critique of the Gotha Programme," pp. 568–569 in McLellan, *Selected Writings*.
22. Many clichéd phrases and ideas that are attributed to Marx were actually the focus of his critique rather than what he was proposing.

REFERENCES

Freire, P. (1972). *Pedagogy of the Oppressed.* Harmondsworth: Penguin.

Gramsci, A. (1971). *Selections from the Prison Notebooks of Antonio Gramsci*, edited and translated by Quintin Hoare and Geoffrey Nowell Smith. London: Lawrence and Wishart.

Mandel, E. (1988). "The Perils of Marketization." *New Left Review*, No. 169 (May/June), 108–120.

Marx, K. (1843a). "On the Jewish Question." In D. McLellan (Ed.), *Karl Marx: Selected Writings* (pp. 39–62). Oxford: Oxford University Press, 1977.

Marx, K. (1843b). "Critique of Hegel's 'Philosophy of Right.'" Extracts in D. McLellan (Ed.), *Karl Marx: Selected Writings* (pp. 26–35). Oxford: Oxford University Press, 1977.

Marx, K. (1844a). "On James Mill." In D. McLellan (Ed.), *Karl Marx: Selected Writings* (pp. 114–123). Oxford: Oxford University Press, 1977.

Marx, K. (1844b). *Economic and Philosophical Manuscripts.* Extracts in D. McLellan (Ed.), *Karl Marx: Selected Writings* (pp. 75–111). Oxford: Oxford University Press, 1977.

Marx, K. (1844c). "Towards a Critique of Hegel's *Philosophy of Right*: Introduction." In D. McLellan (Ed.), *Karl Marx: Selected Writings* (pp. 63–74). Oxford: Oxford University Press, 1977.

Marx, K. (1845). "Theses on Feuerbach." In D. McLellan (Ed.), *Karl Marx: Selected Writings* (pp. 156–158). Oxford: Oxford University Press, 1977.

Marx, K. (1858). *Grundrisse,* translated and with a Foreword by Martin Nicolaus. Harmondsworth: Penguin, 1973.

Marx, K. (1863). *The Theories of Surplus Value.* London: Lawrence and Wishart, Part I, 1967; Part II, 1969; Part III, 1972.

Marx, K. (1865). *Capital,* Vol. 3, translated by David Fernbach, Introduction by Ernest Mandel. Harmondsworth: Penguin, 1981.

Marx, K. (1867). *Capital,* Vol. 1, translated by Ben Fowkes, Introduction by Ernest Mandel. Harmondsworth: Penguin, 1976.

Marx, K. (1869). "On Trade Unions." In D. McLellan (Ed.), *Karl Marx: Selected Writings* (p. 538). Oxford: Oxford University Press, 1977.

Marx, K. (1871). *The Civil War in France.* Extracts in D. McLellan (Ed.), *Karl Marx: Selected Writings* (drafts by Marx, pp. 539–558). Oxford: Oxford University Press, 1977.

Marx, K. (1872). "Preface to the Second German Edition of the Communist Manifesto." In D. McLellan (Ed.), *Karl Marx: Selected Writings* (p. 559–560). Oxford: Oxford University Press, 1977.

Marx, K. (1875). "Critique of the Gotha Programme." In D. McLellan (Ed.), *Karl Marx: Selected Writings* (pp. 564–570). Oxford: Oxford University Press, 1977.

Marx, K. (1878). *Capital,* Vol. 2, translated by David Fernbach, Introduction by Ernest Mandel. Harmondsworth: Penguin, 1978.

Marx, K. (1881). "Letter to Domela-Nieuwhenhuis." In D. McLellan (Ed.), *Karl Marx: Selected Writings* (p. 593–594). Oxford: Oxford University Press, 1977.

Marx, K., and Engels, F. (1845). *The Holy Family.* London: Lawrence and Wishart, 1956.

Marx, K., and Engels, F. (1846). *The German Ideology.* Extracts in D. McLellan (Ed.), *Karl Marx: Selected Writings* (pp. 159–191). Oxford: Oxford University Press, 1977.

Marx, K., and Engels, F. (1848). *The Communist Manifesto.* In D. McLellan (Ed.), *Karl Marx: Selected Writings* (pp. 221–247). Oxford: Oxford University Press, 1977.

Simon, B. (1965). *Education and the Labour Movement 1870–1920.* London: Lawrence and Wishart.

Wright, A. (1983). *British Socialism.* London: Longman.

3

Consciousness

> The whole character of a species, its generic character is contained in its manner of vital activity, and free conscious activity is the species characteristic of [human beings]. . . . [They have] a conscious vital activity. . . . Conscious vital activity differentiates [humans] immediately from animal vital activity.
>
> Marx, 1844, p. 82[1]

Consciousness is one of Marx's central concerns, and it is a central theme in this book too. In the text quoted above, Marx borrows the concept of "alienation" from the German philosopher G. W. F. Hegel to go on to explain how "free conscious activity" had become primarily unfree (Marx, 1844, p. 102).[2]

Our consciousness is comprised of thoughts, ideas and concepts. Potentially, this human characteristic should allow us first to conceive our goals and then to plan and direct our activity toward realizing them. Every animal species also has a specific manner of vital activity, and in the case of some species, such as bees, they perform highly complex and intricate behaviors. However, these behaviors are instinctual; they are genetically programmed. The bee cannot choose to do other than it does. Therefore, we can say that animals, other than humans, cannot escape their nature; they are submerged in their nature. To some extent, humans, prior to developing a scientific understanding of the natural world, had also been submerged, although in a different way, in nature. As a consequence they invented or accepted myths that explained its uncontrollable forces. Marx thought that human consciousness was no longer submerged in this way, or need not be, but instead was submerged in the social formation. People were born into certain relations and conditions that they accepted as natural. Their conscious vital activity was aimed at reproducing these conditions, not at freely, consciously choosing them or some alternative (Marx and Engels, 1846, pp. 52–53).[3] Every major work by Marx deals explicitly or implicitly with analyzing the nature and production of the "unfree" conscious vital activity of human beings (e.g. Marx, 1863, Part III; 1867; Marx and Engels, 1846).

CONCEPTS AND CONSCIOUSNESS

Concepts lie at the foundation of our ideas and thought—our consciousness. Concept formation, as a consequence, is an important subject in developmental psychology. The ability to form concepts only develops midway through the period of childhood. Contemporary psychologists consider concept formation to be an advance in a person's development; therefore, concepts, as such, are treated unproblematically. Marx, however, was well aware of the inherent limitations of human concept formation. I can best explain these limitations by drawing upon certain aspects of Jean Piaget's explanation of child development (Piaget, 1970). Piaget is considered by many people to be the "father" of developmental psychology.

During infant development, each of us begins to make a certain sort of sense of the world as we learn to distinguish between the myriad shapes, colors, sizes, objects and people that present themselves to our senses. But the meaning that is initially created is carried in our activity rather than our minds. Think about the variety of shape-toys that are available for the 6- to 12-month age group, and picture a child's first frustrating attempts to plug the square shape into the circular hole. Soon, however, the child begins to put each shape into the appropriate space and by so doing has taken one of the first steps in bringing some order to her or his experience. At this stage, the child's concept of square or circle is not a mental concept but an action concept. It will take further time for these action concepts to become fully internalized mental concepts that can be linked to words or symbols and reexternalized or communicated by them. However, it is at this early stage of action concepts where we can most clearly understand a point that is central to Marx's theory of consciousness.

Very simply, Marx says that concepts and ideas are not as we think them to be, viz. reflections of "things." Instead they arise from definite relations between people, or between people and objects or objects and objects (e.g. Marx 1847, 1867; Marx and Engels, 1845, 1846). This will become clearer later, but for the moment just think about the infant's repeated activity with the shape-toys. How does the action concept form and become permanent? At first, the play activity may seem random, but soon it develops into activity seeking a relation between the shape object and the shape space. Therefore, even this action concept has been formed not from a singular "thing"—that is, the shape object or, alternatively, the shape space—but rather from the relation between them. Nevertheless, the nature of human language is such that once we have formed internalized mental concepts, we communicate them by means of words or labels that serve to extinguish their relational origins. So while concepts are absolutely essential to us in ordering our experience, we must also be aware of their limitations, especially when we use them in developing a more critical and complex understanding of our social reality. We still will need concepts, but we will also need to understand them and use them critically. And we need a more fluid or less static way of expressing them. I will say more on this later.

MARX'S CRITIQUE OF OTHER THEORIES OF CONSCIOUSNESS

Marx's theory of the formation of ideas, his theory of consciousness, developed from his recognition of the limitations in other theories that were prevalent in the 1840s and before. Marx's academic background was philosophy; therefore, early on most of his writings focused on philosophical thought. At that time, philosophical thinking fell into two broad categories or paradigms, viz. idealism and materialism. Marx was critical of both, and in collaboration with Frederick Engels he set out to develop a distinctive form of materialism.

Marx pursued his academic studies in Germany, where the dominant philosophical paradigm was idealism. His critical writings began with a critique of idealism. According to this critique, any form of idealism assumes that ideas are temporally prior to reality—that is, the real or material world. In *The Holy Family*, Marx parodies idealist philosophy as follows:

> If from real apples, pears, strawberries, and almonds I form the general idea "Fruit", if I go further and imagine that my abstract idea "Fruit", derived from real fruit, is an entity outside me, is indeed the true essence of the pear, the apple, etc.; then, in the language of speculative philosophy I am declaring that "Fruit" is the substance of the pear, the apple, the almond, etc. . . . what is essential to these things is not their real being . . . but the essences that I have extracted from them, and then foisted on them, the essence of my idea—"Fruit". . . . If apples, pears, almonds and strawberries are really nothing but "Substance", "Fruit", the question arises: Why does "Fruit" manifest itself to me sometimes as an apple, sometimes as a pear, sometimes as an almond? Why this appearance of diversity which so strikingly contradicts my speculative conception of "Unity"; "Substance"; "Fruit"? . . .
>
> This, answers the speculative philosopher, is because fruit is not dead, undifferentiated, motionless, but living, self differentiating, moving. [Marx and Engels, 1845, pp. 135–136][4]

Marx makes the idealism of speculative philosophy sound quite absurd, and readers might think that idealism was a problem confined to nineteenth-century speculative philosophy. However, I would argue that idealism is "alive and thriving" in many aspects of late twentieth-century thought. The main characteristics of idealism are the separation of ideas from the material world and then the designation of them as the creators or causes of real phenomena. Modern variations of these characteristics can be observed in certain uses of concepts, such as intelligence, personality, motivation, femininity and masculinity—to name but a few.

As mentioned previously, Marx was also critical of materialism. He considered the materialism he criticized to be simply a reversal of idealism. It held that the real or material world was the origin of ideas; ideas were the mechanical efflux of real phenomena. In the 1840s, Marx was drawn to the critique of religious thought which had been promulgated by the materialist philosopher Feuerbach. Feuerbach argued that God was a creation of the human mind, but a creation that had obtained a separate existence from its creator: hence a form of idealism. In the same way that the "Fruit" was the essence of the apple, God had become the essence, the creator, of human beings. Although Marx thought that this was a very good explanation of the origins of religious thinking, he was critical of Feuerbach's materialism (Marx, 1845).[5]

For Marx the problem with both idealism and materialism was that they created a dualism, a separation or dichotomy, between thought and reality. Once these are thought of as separate and distinct, then primacy can be assigned to one or the other. This was ironical to Marx because the dualism of both idealism and materialism led to a reified way of thinking that he sometimes characterized as "thingness" (Marx and Engels, 1846, pp. 42, 67–70).[6] Marx thought that the real world and consciousness should be understood as a relation rather than as separate "things."

For Marx, the real world was, and always would be, changing and developing, and therefore it was historically specific. He criticized reified thinking because it produced concepts that ignored and therefore lacked historical specificity (p. 43).[7] Such concepts were then used to understand the past as well as the present and future, thus constituting a framework for all knowledge and understanding. Despite their apparent differences, therefore, idealism and mechanical or ahistorical materialism produced identical theories of knowledge or epistemologies. Knowledge could either be discovered through the empirical observation of the given, unchanging real world or grasped once and for all by the correct philosophical thinking about the world, but in either case it came to assume a separate existence from reality.

MARX'S MATERIALISM AND HIS MATERIALIST THEORY OF CONSCIOUSNESS

In contrast to other theories, Marx's materialism (which I touched on briefly in chapter 2) postulated that ideas and concepts arise from relations between people and from relations between people and their material world (the world created by human beings as well as the natural world). The "thingness" or reification that characterized philosophical thinking—and, as I discuss below, a great deal of bourgeois thought in general—was produced by thinking about the result of the relation, or only one aspect of the relation, rather than about the relation itself. According to Marx we actively and sensuously experience these relations; therefore, our consciousness is actively produced within our experience of our social, material and natural existence (Marx and Engels,

1846, pp. 41–43).[8] Furthermore, these relations and experiences are historically specific. In *The German Ideology,* Marx and Engels argued that if you wanted to understand the prevailing form of consciousness in any social formation (e.g. feudalism or capitalism) the place to start was with real people and their activity, but especially the activity that took place within the way they were organized to produce and reproduce their material existence. This activity takes place within historically specific relations, and these relations are the key not only to people's consciousness but to what they are like as human beings.

> This mode of production must not be considered simply as being the reproduction of the physical existence of these individuals. Rather it is a definite form of activity of these individuals, a definite form of expressing their lives, a definite *mode of life* on their part. As individuals express their life, so they are. What they are, therefore, coincides with their production, both with *what* they produce and with *how* they produce. [Marx and Engels, 1846, p. 37][9]

As a consequence what we are as human beings, our "human nature," does not preexist these relations but is formed historically within them. It is worth pointing out that this remains, to this day, a revolutionary and extremely challenging concept of "human nature." For Marx and Engels, the problem so far in human history was that people had not critically and creatively planned these relations but had accepted those that they were born into as natural and inevitable (p. 53).[10] The relations of feudalism and capitalism, every distinct social formation, are the actual lived relations within which we produce and reproduce our material existence, but so far in history some people have produced that material existence while others have commanded the fruits of their labor. Marx and Engels also stressed that the relations within which we reproduced our species are important to our consciousness and to what we were, in total as human beings (pp. 48–49).[11] Here, of course, they were referring to the historically specific relations of the family and, more generally, to those between women and men.

We have already seen, in their critique of philosophy, a critique that Marx, in particular, was to extend to the general characteristics of bourgeois thought, the consciousness of the capitalist social formation. If thought tended to focus on the results of relations rather than on the relations themselves, it would lead to a fragmented or partial consciousness, or way of thinking, that prevented people from forming a true understanding of their reality. Marx referred to this type of thinking or consciousness as ideology or ideological thought, and therefore his theory of consciousness contains a critical or negative concept of ideology (Larrain, 1983). As mentioned earlier, Marx drew upon Hegel's concept of alienation, but he also developed it to explain how this tendency toward ideological thought was the result of people's activity.

According to Marx's interpretation, Hegel thought that people were alienated from their "species-being" because they did not realize that reality was a creation of their own self's consciousness, and he thought that Hegel was implying that the only thing people had to do was to recognize the connection and then they would overcome alienation (Marx, 1844, p. 102).[12] Alienation, for Marx, could not be overcome by any amount of thinking because its origin was not in thought but the relation between thought and human practice. Human beings objectify their powers and activity in the material world they produce. They produce a world of objects with a separate existence from themselves; however, there is nothing inherently wrong with or alienating about this objectification (pp. 78 ff.).[13] The source of alienation lies within the social relations of human practice that allow some people to decide what is to be produced and to control the results of production, while others become no more than objects to be used in the production process and dominated by the very powers they have externalized through their labor (Marx, 1858, pp. 831–832). Although alienation has no psychological origins, it can have real psychological impact on our consciousness as well as on our subjective well-being.

From what has been said so far, it is hopefully obvious that even in his earliest critiques Marx had begun to formulate a new theory of consciousness and one that included a negative or critical concept of ideology or ideological thought and explanation. It was the ideas and concepts formed within the limited relations of capitalism, but divorced from their relational source, that would become the raw material for ideological explanations, or what today some people call discourses. Although Marx's theory of consciousness, which made his materialism distinctive, and his critical concept of ideology were expressed, in collaboration with Engels, as early as 1846 in *The German Ideology* (a work not published until 1932), their full scientific and theoretical explanation depended upon Marx's subsequent understanding and presentation of the dialectical nature of capitalism. Therefore, by 1846 Marx had developed a distinctive form of materialism that allowed for no separation of consciousness and human reality/practice. Social consciousness was inseparable from social being. His materialism offered a revolutionary theory of "being" (ontology) and a revolutionary theory of knowledge (epistemology) because it related these two theories—that is, demonstrated their *inner* connection. To ignore this can lead to what I am sure Marx would have called a bourgeois reading of his analysis of capitalism.[14]

That sort of reading, even when done by critics of capitalism, would focus only on the creation and distribution of wealth (a *materialistic* focus) and thereby would ignore the fact that Marx also was explaining the material basis of bourgeois consciousness and its dominant tendency to reflect ideological processes of thinking which fragment, partialize, abstract from relational origins and thus serve to distort one's understanding of reality.

Once Marx had formulated a theory of consciousness that posited the inseparable unity of active existence with thought, he had created a theory of praxis (rather than simply one of consciousness) that linked thought and action. Whereas the term praxis is often used to refer to an application of theory to practice (or vice versa), Marx's theory intimately relates—dialectically relates—all thought with practice. His theory also implicitly distinguishes between limited or reproductive praxis and critical or revolutionary praxis, and this is a distinction I use throughout this book.[15]

Therefore, according to Marx, praxis—the unity of thought and action or active experience—is transhistorical. This means that this theory of praxis explains human consciousness throughout the entirety of human existence. However, praxis, its exact form, is also historically specific.[16] I discuss this in detail later; however, for now, it is important to note that socialists or anyone working for social transformation must distinguish between the praxis of bourgeois society and that which would be appropriate for a just and humane form of human existence.

MARX'S CRITIQUE OF THE BOURGEOIS CONCEPT OF THE INDIVIDUAL AND THE STATE

Even before undertaking his analysis of the capitalist economy, Marx was able to shed considerable light on the limited or reproductive praxis of bourgeois society through his analysis of how the individual and the state were conceptualized.

Any concept is based on attributes. For example, we all hold a concept of a "dog," and all the animals that fit our concept will share common attributes such as fur, four legs, wet noses, etc. The content or attributes of our concepts will vary not only historically but according to cultural and subcultural practices. In some cultures, for example, dogs are thought of as wild animals, whereas in others they are domesticated animals. Even within a single culture that has domesticated the dog, different subcultural practices lead to some groups thinking of dogs as working animals and others to thinking of them as pets.

Marx thought that the bourgeois concept of the individual was a very limited one. It was limited because only one attribute really defined a person as a human individual, viz. choice or will. At least according to bourgeois thought, status as a human individual seemed to be threatened only if people were prevented from exercising their choice or will—when the exercise of this attribute was thwarted (Marx and Engels, 1846, pp. 96–101).[17] Obviously individuals could be conceptualized quite differently. They could be conceived of as resplendent in attributes, as Marx thought they would be in a communist social formation. Another way of saying this is that they would be rich in needs (Marx, 1858, p. 325).[18] To deprive a person of expressing any one of this array of attributes could not be tolerated in the type of communist society that Marx advocated because to do so would mean treating a person as less than human.

Although Marx held that the individual of the future would be rich in attributes, his critique of the bourgeois concept of the individual was focused on one particular missing attribute that he felt was essential. This was the attribute of political activity. Under representative democracies, which Marx thought were the most appropriate political organizations for bourgeois societies, people divest their political power and activity, their choices, their decisions and the execution of political activities, in other people. As I said in chapter 2, for Marx, socialism and communism had to entail a relocation of "politics" within the day-to-day activity of all people. Its alienation would be an affront and a serious threat to one's status as a human being.

Since political activity is not a necessary attribute of the bourgeois individual, politics is considered to be a separate sphere of life. In an article, "On the Jewish Question," Marx (1843) argued that it was only with the emergence of bourgeois society that civil society and the state came to be experienced as, and therefore conceptualized as, separate spheres of human society. This remains true of our own experience. For the vast majority of people, the activity of life takes place within the organizations and relations of civil society—the family, church, trade union, work, and so forth. What we do not directly take part in is government. Furthermore, political struggle that takes place outside the framework of the local or national state, although tolerated so long as it offers no effective challenge, is not considered legitimate politics. Marx thought that the bourgeois concept of the state as well as its actual functioning was, and would remain, a historically specific feature of capitalism. As usual with Marx, there had to be a material and historical reason for the development of this separation and for the tendency to experience and so think of aspects of life that, in fact, were related as separate and distinct. Therefore, he turned his attention to an analysis of the material reality of capitalism and its historical development to offer an explanation of both the capitalist economy and the ideological processes of thinking, which tend to arise from people's experiences within capitalist societies.

MARX'S ANALYSIS OF THE CAPITALIST ECONOMY

To understand the way in which bourgeois praxis is limited and reproductive and to understand, thereby, the origins of ideological thinking processes, such as abstraction, separation and partial focusing, we need to consider certain aspects of Marx's analysis of capitalism. I will begin with the overarching structure of his economic works and then focus more precisely on the development of the relations that he presents in the first volume of *Capital*. These are the essence of capitalism.

Marx does not use the term "ideology" often in his economic writings; however, the sense of that term together with a materialist explanation of its source is one of the primary concerns in these writings (especially Marx, 1858, 1863, 1865, 1867). Marx does not claim that all thinking within bourgeois society is ideological, only that there is a tendency toward people developing this type of consciousness. This tendency is due to the way in which consciousness is actively produced within capitalism. *If thought tends to divide and separate* that which, in fact, is related or interdependent, *it is because we experience the components of the relation in a different space and at a different time*

(Marx, 1858, p. 148).[19] For example, as I previously indicated, the motor force or goal of production under capitalism is the creation of profit and the accumulation of capital. Marx carefully explains, and I go into this later, how the basis of profit—viz. surplus value—is created in production and sometimes added to within circulation but that commodities pregnant with this surplus must be exchanged if profit is to be realized (Marx, 1858, pp. 415–418).[20] Therefore, profit depends upon the unity, the relation, between production and exchange. Since even the workers who produce a certain commodity have no claim to it, most of everyone's experience of commodities occurs within the sphere of exchange. Marx called this the "noisy sphere" because it is within market relations that all the ideas that justify the system originate (Marx, 1867, pp. 279–280).[21] Ideas such as equality, freedom and individual choice were originally related to market exchange and only later slightly modified when they were adopted within limited forms of democratic theory and practice (Hall, 1982).

We also tend to think that profit is derived from exchange, in part because some profit continues to be redistributed between middlemen and merchants in the sphere of exchange. However, the redistribution of money from one person's pockets to another's is only a secondary source of profit-making under capitalism and also predates the capitalist social form. Marx's whole economic analysis pivoted around discovering and then explaining how the phenomenon, M (money) becomes M′ (money with augmented value). One person becoming wealthier by outdealing another or the adage "buying cheap and selling dear" cannot account for M becoming M′ or for the overall growth of capital. Marx explained the phenomenon M′ by dialectically establishing the necessary relation between production and exchange. However, to do this he had to grasp and then explain an even more essential relation between labor power and capital (Marx, 1867, pp. 247–280).[22]

To establish that this essential relation between labor power and capital was the result of history, Marx begins the first volume of *Capital* with an analysis of the development of the commodity form (1867, chap. 1).

According to Marx, a commodity is comprised of two values: use-value and exchange-value (p. 126). However the *products* of human labor only acquire the second value and become *commodities* when human beings produce a surplus (in terms of the producer's needs) and therefore are able to engage in exchange or trade with one another. If one person produces a surplus of a useful product, say shoes, and another produces a surplus of, say, wheat, then they can exchange these surpluses with each other. But how do they decide how many pairs of shoes should be exchanged for, say, one bushel of wheat? Marx reasoned that these products must share something in common that will establish their respective exchange-value. Certainly, both have a use, but the use is specific to each and therefore cannot be the common factor. The labor skill (concrete labor) used to produce them is also specific to each, so neither can it be the common factor (p. 128). Marx explains that the only factor shared by all commodities and which therefore can establish their equivalency is the labor time (abstract labor) it takes to produce them (p. 129). However, this cannot be the specific amount of time used to produce the shoes or wheat because that will vary according to the particular skills and conditions of each producer. Exchange equivalency must therefore be based on an average. The average will pertain to the time it takes on average within certain social and historical conditions to produce a pair of shoes or a bushel of wheat. Marx called this the "socially necessary labour time" (p. 129).

As trade developed and the division of labor increased so that the producer of shoes was exchanging his or her surplus for many surpluses other than just the wheat, one commodity became a universal equivalent for all the others. This universal equivalent facilitated exchange. Instead of having to establish the exchange-value between shoes and every other product individually, which could involve a great deal of haggling and the breakdown in many transactions, each individual commodity became related to the universal one (p. 162). During the early development of exchange relations, the universal equivalent might have been a commodity such as wheat or cattle, but as exchange grew in both quantity and spatial scope, a more flexible and durable equivalent was needed.

Marx details the history through which gold and silver developed into the universal equivalents and the money form (especially Marx, 1858, pp. 165–186). We tend to forget that gold and silver are extracted from nature by human labor and circulated throughout the world by other types of human labor. Therefore, like any other commodity, they are produced in a certain amount of socially necessary labor time. If they were not, they could not be used to establish equivalency with other commodities. They would share no common factor. It should also be noted that once the products of human labor acquire this second value, the exchange-value, people will tend to experience the two values at a different time and in a different place. However, the separate experience of exchange-value and use-value only becomes problematical under the capitalist social formation (Marx, 1867, pp. 270–280).[23] To understand fully why it becomes problematical, we need to consider some of the differences between feudalism and capitalism.

Under feudalism, the productive workers—the serfs—produced all their own necessities, and they also produced a surplus for the lord of the manor. The serfs could clearly see what they had produced for themselves and the surplus they had to produce for someone else, especially, as was often the case, when production for these separate purposes took place at a separate time and place. In exchange, the lord was to provide protection for the serf, and their different positions within society were justified by a religious form of ideology that made clear the different, allegedly God-given, rights and responsibilities of each class. This ideology did not need to mask the contradictions of reality; in fact, it could not, because they were clearly visible (p. 680). However, it did need to justify them.

Gradually the feudal social formation and its overt form of social domination gave way to the production and exchange of commodities and the capitalist social form, and this new form of production required new labor conditions. Marx argues that capitalism depended on the emergence of a "free" wage laborer. Workers had to be free in two senses. They no longer were bonded by duty or obligation but were free to sell their labor each day or week. In fact, this was the only thing they could sell in order to obtain their own necessities because, with the breakup of feudal relations, people no longer had land or tools to produce these. This was the second sense in which they had become free (pp. 272–273). Capitalism only emerged when the investment of a particular amount of money produced an augmented value. Marx explains that money acquires this augmented value and thereby becomes capital by purchasing a very special commodity that has a very special use-value. Labor power was (and is) this very special commodity (p. 270).

Marx analyzed the commodity, labor power, in terms of the two values that make up every commodity. The exchange-value is the wage, and the use-value is labor that can create value, and, moreover, value greater than its own exchange-value (p. 283). This labor, of course, also creates use-values with exchange-values —commodities—but these are important only as the material or objectified expression of value. Market exchanges are supposed to be based on the exchange of equivalents; therefore, the wage should be equivalent to the use-value it purchases. However, Marx argues that under capitalist relations of production this particular exchange of equivalents is only an appearance. If we focus only on exchange, we cannot see why labor power provides such a very important use-value for capital. Therefore Marx takes us "behind" the appearance of equality and into the production process (pp. 279 ff.).

In his examination of the production process, Marx explains that value-creating labor is also comprised of two parts. He refers to the two parts as paid and unpaid labor, or alternatively, necessary and surplus labor. The paid or necessary labor is the labor time it takes to produce enough commodities to produce, once sold, the wage that makes it possible for workers to buy their necessities. But capitalists could hardly stay in business if they did not also use labor power to produce a surplus that accrues to capital. Therefore, some of the labor must be unpaid or surplus labor, and it is this surplus labor that impregnates commodities with the surplus value that is the basis of capitalist profit (p. 325).[24] Just how capitalists go about extracting this surplus from labor power varies at different times and places. Sometimes it involves simply extending the working day, whereas at others it involves using production techniques, technology or management styles to work labor more intensively, thereby increasing surplus labor even within a working day of fixed duration. When capitalists refer to labor productivity, they are actually referring to increasing the *ratio* between paid and unpaid labor so that each commodity produced contains less of the former in relation to the latter. Since it is the ratio between the two that is important, it can even be increased while wages are rising. Therefore, it is possible to have a high level of wages and a high level of exploitation (i.e., rate of surplus value) at the same time (p. 753).[25] It is important to understand that the unequal exchange between labor and capital can only be corrected by abolishing the labor–capital relation or the social relation of capitalist production. This unequal exchange is the bourgeois practice that was at loggerheads with the principles of commodity exchange mentioned in chapter 2.[26]

As indicated earlier, Marx's analysis of the capitalist production process, the capitalist relations of production, also involves an explanation of how the experience of capitalism leads to an ideological understanding of how the system works (pp. 163–177).[27] I have noted that the production of a surplus under feudalism was clearly visible for all to see; however, under capitalism the impregnation of commodities with surplus value is less than obvious. The necessary capitalist relation—that is, the inseparable unity between labor and capital—is masked by our real-life experiences. However, Marx demonstrates that capital could not be augmented value without using labor power as it does and that wage laborers can only come to have one life-sustaining commodity to sell (i.e. their labor power) within their relation to capital (p. 724).[28] But this is not how we experience or think about the laborer's commodity. First of all, workers do not sell their laboring capacity to engage in "conscious vital activity," to work and create, but rather to acquire a wage by which they can live. Struggles about wages usually revolve around the amount and whether it is a "fair" amount for the labor expended, not the wage relation itself or the special use-value that their labor power provides for capital. The focus of attention is on the exchange-value of labor. Therefore, the separation, in experience and thus thought, of the two values of this commodity means that the special use-value is ignored, and therefore most people understand little about, or only a partial aspect of, the relations that make the capitalist system possible.

As consumers, workers, in the first instance, also encounter other commodities as exchange-values. A particular commodity could be the most essential or useful thing in the world, but no matter how much it is needed it is the exchange-value that will determine whether you have it. This is even true for the workers who have produced that commodity. But, for the most part, the vast majority of commodities that workers buy, or desire to buy, are not the ones they produce, and this distances them even further from an awareness of how the commodity's value is constituted. However, unlike those who are not as yet embroiled in a wage relation that produces surplus value, workers within this relation will have at least some subjective knowledge of the exploitation they experience. Marx was trying to provide everyone with a dialectical (often he calls this scientific) knowledge of these processes.

We need this sort of knowledge because the process of impregnating a commodity with a surplus value during production which can only become of real benefit to capital when it is sold at a separate time and place is a complex process that we experience in a fragmented manner, and this leads to a distorted, an ideological, way of thinking about commodities. We tend to think that we pay the price we do because of some intrinsic attribute or property of a commodity. Therefore, in our consciousness we conceive of a relation between a commodity and a certain amount of money. In other words, we think of a relation between things that in reality only results from a relation between people, viz. the labor–capital relation. And even that relation is conceived as a thing, viz. the wage (pp. 163–177).[29]

If we consider the actual experience of capitalism from the standpoint of capital (either the individual capitalist or capital that is jointly owned), what is happening is equally, if not more, obscured (p. 682).[30] Although I do not go into great detail about this here, one problem has to do with the movements, or investments, of capital brought about by the competition between capitalist firms. These movements tend to create an average rate of profit, which means that the profit that accrues to each capital is based on the total amount of surplus value produced by all the separate capitalist firms rather than on the specific value produced by each (Marx, 1865).[31] In addition, each capitalist, or any particular capital, has paradoxical motives with reference to wages. Since capital needs consumers, it is in the interest of each capitalist enterprise for the wages paid by all the others to be as high as possible. Therefore, at one and the same time each capitalist firm must encourage most workers to spend, but its own must be encouraged to accept low wages and to be frugal (Marx, 1858, pp. 419–420). Capitalists seem quite aware that they must encourage their own work force to work more efficiently to increase productivity; they know that this will affect their profits. However, this is more a knowledge based on experience than one based on an analysis or critical understanding of what is actually taking place.

As capitalism develops, it comes to be based on an even greater division of labor (Marx, 1867, pp. 456–491).[32] This means that instead of several workers each producing a complete commodity, many workers produce some aspect of the final commodity. Therefore, even the worker or capitalist who had read Marx would find it difficult to know just how much labor was producing the wage and, alternatively, just how much the surplus. Capitalists and workers alike often understand the system in terms of the ideological explanations that have filtered into common sense from the bourgeois economists' analyses of the surface features or phenomena of capitalism. The system is explained by attributing special qualities to capital, or to its personification, the capitalist. "Money makes money," or the idea that entrepreneurs are imbued with certain personality attributes that produce wealth, are two of the most familiar of these common-sense notions (pp. 254–257). As with the notion of "market forces," there is a bit of magic at play here. This type of explanation never explains "how" but demands a leap of imagination. Furthermore, we only accept these tidbits of common sense if, in the first instance, we focus on a partial or fragmented view of the total process and the part we play in reproducing it. But then Marx emphasized that if the relations we need to understand—the social contradictions—were there for us plainly to view, we would not need "science," or, rather, a dialectical conceptualization that enables us to penetrate the surface phenomena of capitalism (p. 433).[33]

The section in Volume 1 of *Capital* that traces the development of the commodity form ends with an explanation of the type of ideological thought that will result as a consequence of the full development of the commodity form under capitalism. I previously mentioned that we tend to think that the value of a commodity derives from its own intrinsic properties. Perhaps the best examples of this are gold and gems, which seem to radiate these properties. We forget that like all other commodities they share the common factor that they are produced (i.e. extracted from nature) and circulated for exchange by a certain amount of socially necessary labor time. Capitalist praxis and the ideological explanations that arise from it and serve to justify the system encourage us to think about commodities in a distorted way. However, even worse, according to Marx, these ideological processes become located in our subjective responses. We come to desire, even lust after, commodities or possessions. Marx calls this the "commodity fetish," the subjective or emotional location of bourgeois ideology (pp. 163–177).

As we all know, the aim of human existence increasingly has become the possession of more and more "things." Human beings often are treated and treat one another as commodities, possessions, and, further, as easily disposable ones once their use has been consumed. Our needs and desires are defined, and so we tend to define them in terms of commodities. When the pursuit of "things" becomes the goal of human existence, it also increasingly defines the organizational basis for the vast majority of our experience. In the conclusion to this chapter, I explain some of the effects of these tendencies on education.

One of the most crucial points that Marx tries to explain to us is that we live an existence wherein we relate to "things," an existence that conceals the fact that humans are interdependent, social beings (pp. 163–177).[34] The development of the division of labor coupled with the bourgeois ideology of individualism may make people feel that they are separate and autonomous, but, in fact, with the development of an international, global division of labor, people have become even more dependent on one another. For Marx, this dependence or interdependence of human beings holds the potential for uniting humankind; however, it remains only a potential in the absence of the development of our "species-being," viz. a *free* conscious vital activity or, in other words, critical/revolutionary praxis (pp. 617–619).[35]

USING CONCEPTS CRITICALLY

I have pointed out that concepts are essential to us because they help us make sense of and order our experience. Nevertheless, hopefully it now is clear that revolutionary or socialist praxis must depend upon our ability to use concepts critically. However, if our concepts and consciousness, in general, arise from our active experience within definite social relations and other material conditions, and if under capitalism these are limited so that we think of things as separate and unrelated, how can we break through these distortions in our psychological processes and think more critically? How did Marx do it? These are crucial questions for developing critical, socialist and eventually revolutionary praxis. However, I must once more emphasize that using concepts critically will not, in itself, change anything. Nevertheless, it is a necessary first step in working out strategies for social transformation. Unfortunately it is a step that has frequently been ignored.

To reiterate: both before and after Marx, a tendency with a great deal of socialist thought and practice has been to challenge the results of the fundamental relations of capitalism rather than the relations themselves. The result, instead of the relation, is grasped mentally as a concept and then energy is directed at defeating the symptoms while leaving the causes intact. To avoid this tendency, we need to look in further detail at what Marx did with bourgeois concepts.

In the introduction to the *Grundrisse*, Marx parodies bourgeois concepts such as "production in general" and "consumption in general." He complains that bourgeois thinkers form concepts by observing their own social formation, their present material reality, and, since they are submerged in this social form, they do not realize that their concepts are historically specific. Because they fail to recognize this, they then go on to apply their own concept to the total history of human production, miss out the historical differences—and, as a consequence, historical change—and end up with a concept of human production in general (Marx, 1858, pp. 83–85).[36] Their concepts are transhistorical or equally applicable to the entirety of human history. Transhistorical concepts have a use, but it is a limited one. Marx's own concept of praxis allows us to formulate a generalization about the origin of human consciousness. However, the generalizations that transhistorical concepts allow us to make will become misleading unless they are used in conjunction with historically specific concepts (pp. 83-85).[37] For example, our understanding is enhanced when we distinguish between limited/reproductive praxis and critical/revolutionary praxis or when we establish the historical specificity of capitalist production and consumption, viz. the relations that underpin them.

Transhistorical conceptualization also leads to another problem when used on its own. Since the concepts become divorced from their original historical content, they are extremely abstract. Their degree of abstractness allows those who use them to conflate them. In the example cited above, Marx goes on to parody the conflation of production in general and consumption in general (pp. 90–94). They are just different aspects of the same thing. Production is considered to be the consumption of raw materials, and consumption is the production of need or renewed demand. This conflation of, or immediate identity between, production and consumption (the result of exchange) obliterates the relation between production and exchange and makes it impossible to understand how that relation affects what actually takes place in production and exchange and eventually consumption (pp. 94–100). Therefore conflation works similarly to separation in that it deflects our attention from the relations we need to grasp to understand how the capitalist system actually works.

Inductive and deductive processes of abstraction are employed in forming and then using transhistorical concepts. People observe the attributes of, say, production in their own social formation, inductively form a general concept and then deductively use that concept to seek confirming attributes in other social formations. Differences are ignored. For example, if machines are conceptualized as capital in a capitalist social formation, then the bourgeois thinker assumes that the earliest tools developed by human beings were also capital. Marx thought that this was ridiculous. He stressed that capital arises from specific historical relations; it was not some attribute of a thing. In other words, a machine (or any tool) is just a machine and only becomes capital within historically specific relations (p. 86).[38]

Bourgeois concepts pertain to current phenomena that, according to Marx, are actually historical results. Therefore, if we are to form and use concepts critically, we have to grasp the historically specific relations from which these phenomena arise. We will need to assume, as Marx did, that phenomena, and our concepts of them, originate from relations. Then we need a type of abstraction that enables us to postulate what possible relations might have produced the results we are analyzing (Marx, 1867, pp. 493–494, fn. 4).[39] Derek Sayer (1983) has distinguished Marx's type of abstraction from induction and deduction. He refers to it as retroduction and argues that Marx did not abstract the attributes of the phenomena inductively or deductively test his concepts by reference only to the surface of reality or experience; instead, he penetrated surface phenomena—metaphorically, he conceptually went beneath them (this metaphor is used in Marx, 1867, p. 279). Marx's analysis of capitalism involved penetrating a phenomenon, or a concept of it, to grasp the unity of opposites, the relation, that had made it possible. To conceptualize a phenomenon as a unity of opposites is to assume that it is the result of, or alteratively a part of, a dialectical contradiction (Marx and Engels, 1845, pp. 134–135).[40] Although I explain this in much more detail in the next chapter, I mention it here because Marx's use of concepts and the form of his concepts were dialectical and were crucial to his dialectical explanation of capitalism. While I am sympathetic with Sayer's attempt to distinguish the type of abstraction used by Marx from either induction or deduction, I am not convinced that it is useful to think of retroduction as distinct from dialectical conceptualization.

To understand a phenomenon dialectically, or as a unity of opposites, involves conceptualizing it as composed of two parts that are necessary to each other because they could not exist as they currently do without each other. I have already described how Marx conceptualized abstract labor—the labor that creates value—as comprised of two parts, viz. paid and unpaid labor, and how he presented the development of the commodity form on the basis of its two parts, viz., use-value and exchange-value. In fact, if you think about the aspects of Marx's economics discussed thus far, you can see that he conceptualized all phenomena as being comprised of two parts, as unities of opposites that could not exist without the other. For example, when a product of human labor develops into the commodity form, its use-value cannot exist for us unless it has an exchange-value, and its exchange-value can only be realized if it has some type of use-value. Each of the two parts of the unity, the relation, is constantly moving and developing. I explain why in the next chapter, but for now I can point out that since the existence of each opposite depends upon its relation to the other, a tension is created that in turn determines (when the opposites are, or are related to, conscious beings) whether the opposites attempt to better their position in the relation or, alternatively, attempt to dissolve the relation. Whichever is the case, the tension will create movement. Once the unity of opposites that produces a particular phenomenon has been mentally grasped, then the historical development of the opposites in relation to each other can be traced.

Although I do not want to anticipate prematurely the full discussion of Marx's dialectical conceptualization, which is the focus of chapter 4, I should mention that the aspects of this mode of conceptualization described here are what enabled him to establish the historically specific difference between, for example, capitalist production and the production of material existence in other social formations. It was also, of course, this mode of conceptualization that enabled him to develop a revolutionary theory of consciousness (praxis).

I mentioned previously that Marx parodied the bourgeois tendency to conflate or establish an immediate identity between concepts such as production and consumption. Marx, on the other hand, was trying to understand the true reality of capitalist production and consumption, and to do this he had to conceptualize production and exchange (the *a priori* condition of consumption) as unities or relations, not identities. These unities are the real dialectical social contradictions that reveal the *inner* mechanisms of capitalism. By explaining phenomena as unities of opposites, Marx was not only able to trace their developments historically, he was also able to point out that we usually experience the components of each of these unities separately in time and space. As a consequence, we tend to think of them as separate and unrelated. Alternatively, once we separate them in thought we may equate them or incorrectly conceptualize them as identical.

Marx's dialectical formulation and use of concepts also enabled him to establish the reason for the fundamental and therefore recurrent economic crises experienced under capitalism—that is, the forcible, real separation of the two opposites, which could only be overcome on capitalist terms by reestablishing their unity or relation. In capitalist crises of overproduction, described in chapter 2, the relation between production and exchange can only be rectified by waste and sacrifice. To maintain the profit for some capitalist firms, others and their commodities will have to be destroyed and, as usual, human consumption, which has no purchasing power, will be denied (Marx, 1858, p. 150).[41]

Since one of the central arguments in this book pertains to the importance of education in achieving effective social transformation, it might be useful to round off the discussion thus far of Marx's critical (i.e. dialectical) use of concepts by considering how we might begin to develop a dialectical conceptualization of one aspect of capitalist culture, viz. the bourgeois concept of education.

THINKING DIALECTICALLY ABOUT BOURGEOIS EDUCATION

There is a phenomenon, a historical result, and a concept of it that we call education. It is organized, experienced and conceptualized as a thing or a compilation of things, bodies of knowledge, that some people possess (teachers and experts) and others need to acquire (students or learners). This organization, experience and concept of education can be understood only if we mentally penetrate these surface features and grasp the relations that make them possible. We have to consider concretely, or in reality, how unities of opposites are related and how the nature of these relations has resulted in education as we know and experience it. Teachers and students—the real, live individuals who are actively producing and reproducing the phenomenon, the experience and our concept of it—are the first unity of opposites we should consider. Teachers or experts only exist as the exclusive possessors of knowledge if they are related to students in a way that determines the latter as deficient or devoid of knowledge and therefore dependent on the teacher. Teachers defined as rich in knowledge only exist as such in relation to their opposite—that is, the needy learners. Furthermore, learners can only be considered needy if they are related to an opposite who possesses what the learners need.

However, this relationship between teachers and students actually depends on a more fundamental one. The real, living individuals—teachers and students—are also constituted within a relation to knowledge. This relation should be understood dialectically as another unity of opposites. Knowledge, as the substance of bourgeois education, is also conceptualized as a thing or object, and this knowledge object is often thought of and treated as something separate from and unrelated to human beings. Of course, teachers know that knowledge is produced by human beings, but in day-to-day practice they could not continue to deliver it as a commodity unless they have come to think of it as their own commodity, a commodity as unchanging and unproblematic as a pair of shoes. In short, we relate to knowledge as something to have, to accumulate in the first instance, rather than as something we use, test, question and produce. We also tend to develop a fetish for the qualifications that signify our possession of it. Knowledge can only become a commodity in relation to people if some of those people, what they are, are determined by their possession of knowledge and others by their need for it.

Earlier, I mentioned that one of the problems with socialist critique, both before and after Marx, was that it focused on the results or symptoms of the fundamental relations, rather than on the relations themselves. I want to return to this point briefly to consider how this tendency has manifested itself in socialists' struggles with bourgeois education. Have we not concerned ourselves with struggles for greater access and equal opportunities so that everyone can acquire the educational commodities? Have we not also engaged in attempts to replace one valued knowledge commodity with another or in redefining, more broadly defining, the locations in which we can acquire the knowledge commodities we need? For example, we have argued for the inclusion of "black" history, women's history and Marx's economics, and we have argued that education can take place outside formal institutions, in pubs, cafés and on the shop floor. These are all worthy arguments, but they do not strike at the real heart of the problem, which is the bourgeois concept of and relation to knowledge/education. By saying this, I am not decrying knowledge, only a concept of it and a relation to it that encourage us first to dichotomize the act of acquiring already existing knowledge from the activity of producing new knowledge. It then encourages us to relegate the latter activity to a separate and exclusive existence called research, not education. It is important to note that this critique of bourgeois education can be extended to many other areas of cultural work. Community services, campaign groups' messages and information or political arguments and ideas can all be delivered within these antagonistic relations; alternatively, they can be shared within distinctive socialist relations. It is a political choice that all cultural workers for socialism and social transformation can make. In chapter 5, I return to this point and consider what the struggle at the level of the essential relations, the struggle against ideological (limited/reproductive) praxis, would entail.

However, before that I want to offer a much more detailed explanation of Marx's dialectical conceptualization and understanding of capitalism.

NOTES

1. Alternative source: *Karl Marx and Frederick Engels Collected Works* [hereafter *MECW*], Vol. 3, 1843–44 (London: Lawrence and Wishart, 1975), p. 276.

2. Alternative source: *MECW*, Vol. 3, pp. 276–277.

3. Alternative source: D. McLellan (Ed.), *Karl Marx: Selected Writings* (Oxford: Oxford University Press, 1977), pp. 172–173. Complementary reading: K. Marx, *The Eighteenth Brumaire of Louis Bonaparte*, 1852, pp. 300–325 in McLellan, *Selected Writings*. Further comment: K. Marx and F. Engels, *The German Ideology*, 1846 (Moscow: Progress Publishers); this very important source was not published until 1932.

4. Alternative source: K. Marx and F. Engels, *The Holy Family*, 1845 (London: Lawrence and Wishart, 1956), pp. 78–83.

5. Alternative source: McLellan, *Selected Writings*, pp. 156–158.

6. Complementary readings and comments: K. Marx, *Economic and Philosophical Manuscripts*, 1844, pp. 103, 105 in McLellan, *Selected Writings*. Here he refers to "thingness" or the conversion of something alive and dynamic into a thing; K. Marx, *Theories of Surplus Value*, 1863, Part III (London: Lawrence & Wishart, 1972), pp. 274, 429, also p. 483, where he says: "Capital more and more acquires a material form, is transformed more and more from a relation into a thing." In fact, all three parts of *Theories of Surplus Value* are rich sources for the point I am making here because they are critiques of how bourgeois economists think about capitalism. See also *Capital*, Vol. 1, pp. 982 ff.; *Grundrisse*, pp. 164, 247–249. The sources and pages noted here are only selections, as this is a recurring point in Marx's writings.

7. Alternative source: McLellan, *Selected Writings*, p. 165. Complementary readings: *Grundrisse*, pp. 88 ff.; *Capital*, Vol. 1, "Postface to the 2nd Edition," pp. 100–102; *Theories of Surplus Value*, Part II, p. 44. In these sources, Marx extends his critique to include the thinking of both bourgeois and socialist economists whose analyses were flawed by either idealism or ahistorical materialism.

8. Alternative source: McLellan, *Selected Writings*, p. 164.

9. Alternative source: McLellan, *Selected Writings*, p. 161.

10. Complementary readings: *Grundrisse*, pp. 493–507; *Capital*, Vol. 1, pp. 1063–1065; *Theories of Surplus Value*, Part III, p. 514.

11. Alternative source: McLellan, *Selected Writings*, p. 166.

12. Alternative source: *MECW*, Vol. 3, pp. 335 ff.

13. Alternative source: *MECW*, Vol. 3, pp. 270 ff.

14. I think he would call it this because he criticizes various socialist politicians and economists for thinking about capitalism with the same ideological processes as the bourgeoisie. This is a theme throughout *Theories of Surplus Value* (e.g. Part III, pp. 259 ff.) and also a theme in the *Grundrisse* and in Volumes 1–3 of *Capital*.

15. I arrived at this conclusion independently but later found that it was also proposed by K. Kosík, *Dialectics of the Concrete: A Study of Problems of Man and World* (Dordrecht, Holland: Reidel, 1976). Marx leads the reader most clearly to this conclusion in *Theories of Surplus Value*, Part III, p. 514.

16. I am indebted to Derek Sayer, who alerted me to the importance and significance of these distinctions in Marx's writings. See, for example: D. Sayer, *Marx's Method: Ideology, Science and Critique in "Capital,"* 2nd edition (Brighton: Harvester, 1983), and D. Sayer, *The Violence of Abstraction* (London: Basil Blackwell, 1987). However, in chapter 6, I reclassify this truth as a meta-transhistorical truth and draw a distinction between meta-transhistorical and transhistorical truths.

17. Alternative source: McLellan, *Selected Writings*, pp. 52–54. Complementary reading: K. Marx, "On the Jewish Question," in McLellan, *Selected Writings*, pp. 40–62.

18. Complementary readings: Also in *Grundrisse*, pp. 161–162, 540–542, 831–832; *Economic and Philosophical Manuscripts*, in *MECW*, Vol. 3, p. 304; "On James Mill," in McLellan, *Selected Writings*, pp. 114–123.

19. Complementary readings: This is a point Marx makes throughout his economic writings, but he states it most succinctly on p. 148 of the *Grundrisse*. See also *Grundrisse*, pp. 147–149, 415, 533–537, 544; *Capital*, Vol. 1, p. 209; *Theories of Surplus Value*, Part I, pp. 396, 399, Part II, pp. 500, 504, 505, 508–509, Part III, pp. 120, 485.

20. Complementary readings: *Grundrisse*, pp. 99 ff.; *Capital*, Vol. 3, pp. 353–368; K. Marx, *Capital*, Vol. 2, 1878 (Harmondsworth: Penguin, 1978), pp. 156, 391 fn.

21. Complementary reading: *Grundrisse*, pp. 247–248.

22. Marx first used the concept of labor power and distinguished it from labor in the *Grundrisse*, pp. 281, 282, 293, 359; however, it is comprehensively explained in the citation to *Capital* given here in the text.

23. Complementary readings: *Capital*, Vol. 1, pp. 208–209, 1001–1002, 1058–1065; *Grundrisse*, pp. 266 ff.; *Theories of Surplus Value*, Part I, p. 45. Marx's presentation is historical *and* logical–analytical. This means that the history he depicts is a history of activity that took place only on the margins of pre-capitalist society. The forms he analyzes, like the the commodity and value, only come into their full development in the capitalist social formation.

24. Complementary readings: *Capital*, Vol. 1, pp. 324–326, 975, 1041–1044.

25. Complementary readings and comment: *Capital*, Vol. 1, pp. 320–428 (for full discussion), 432–438, 771–772, 956–959, 1016–1058. The point about the high level of wages is made, as cited in the text, on p. 753.

26. This was the point Marx was making in the "Critique of the Gotha Programme," in McLellan, *Selected Writings*, pp. 564–570. In *Capital*, Vol. 1, see chapters 4 and 5.

27. Complementary readings: *Capital*, Vol. 1, pp. 981–983, 1052 ff.; *Theories of Surplus Value*, Part III, pp. 120, 137, 453, 483, 501, 514.

28. See *Capital*, Vol. I, pp. 724, 724 fn., 1006, for summary or definition.

29. Complementary readings: *Capital*, Vol. 1, pp. 680–682, 1005, 1069–1070; K. Marx, "Wage Labour and Capital" (originally lectures to the Workingmen's Club in Brussels), 1847, in McLellan, *Selected Writings*, pp. 248–268.

30. Complementary readings: *Capital*, Vol. 1, pp. 1052–1058; *Theories of Surplus Value*, Part I, pp. 69, 174, 573, Part III, p. 485.

31. See especially chapters 8, 9 and 10 of *Capital*, Vol. 3. Complementary readings: *Theories of Surplus Value*, Part II, pp. 67–71, 174, Part III, p. 483; *Grundrisse*, pp. 745–767.

32. Complementary reading: *Capital*, Vol. 3, pp. 772–774.

33. Complementary readings: *Capital*, Vol. 1, p. 494 fn.; *Capital*, Vol. 3, p. 956.

34. Complementary reading: *Capital*, Vol. 1, p. 1005. Fetishized and reified thinking are the same forms of thought. They are ideological forms of thought.

35. Complementary readings: *Capital*, Vol. 1, pp. 1052–1055; *Capital*, Vol. 3, pp. 958–959.

36. Complementary readings: *Theories of Surplus Value*, Part I, p. 44; *The German Ideology*, p. 43; McLellan, *Selected Writings*, p. 165.

37. On p. 85 of the *Grundrisse*, Marx says: "However all epochs of production have certain common traits, common characteristics. . . . No production would be thinkable without them; . . . nevertheless, just those things which determine their development, i.e. the elements which are not general or common, must be separated out from the determinations valid for production as such, so that . . . their essential difference is not forgotten. The whole profundity of those modern economists who demonstrated the eternity and harmoniousness of existing social relations lies in this forgetting."

38. Perhaps this is stated with more irony in K. Marx, "Wage Labour and Capital," 1847, p. 256 in McLellan, *Selected Writings*, where Marx says: "A cotton-spinning jenny is a machine for spinning cotton. It becomes capital only in certain relations. Torn from these relationships it is no more capital than gold itself is money."

39. Although it is quite clear throughout Marx's economic writings that he uses a different form of abstraction, this is one place where he makes an implicit reference to it.

40. Complementary readings: *Grundrisse*, pp. 296, 248; *MECW*, Vol. 3, pp. 88–89, 293–294.

41. Complementary readings: *Grundrisse*, pp. 415 ff.; *Capital*, Vol. 3, pp. 357 ff.; *Theories of Surplus Value*, Part II, pp. 500–509.

REFERENCES

Hall, S. (1982). "Managing Conflict, Producing Consent." Unit 21, Block 5: *Conformity, Consensus and Conflict, in D102, Social Sciences: A Foundation Course*. Milton Keynes: Open University Press.

Larrain, J. (1983). *Marxism and Ideology*. London: Macmillan.

Marx, K. (1843). "On the Jewish Question." In D. McLellan (Ed.), *Karl Marx Selected Writings*. Oxford: Oxford University Press, 1977.

Marx, K. (1844). *Economic and Philosophical Manuscripts*. Extracts in D. McLellan (Ed.), *Karl Marx: Selected Writings* (pp. 75–112). Oxford: Oxford University Press, 1977.

Marx, K. (1845). "Addenda: Theses on Feuerbach." In K. Marx and F. Engels, *The German Ideology*. Moscow: Progress Publishers, 1976 edition.

Marx, K. (1847). *The Poverty of Philosophy*. New York: International Publishers, 1969.

Marx, K. (1858). *Grundrisse*. Harmondworth: Penguin, 1973.

Marx, K. (1863). *Theories of Surplus Value*. London: Lawrence and Wishart, Part I, 1967; Part II, 1969; Part III, 1972.

Marx, K. (1865). *Capital*, Vol. 3. Harmondsworth: Penguin, 1981.

Marx, K. (1867). *Capital*, Vol. 1. Harmondsworth: Penguin, 1976.

Marx, K., and Engels, F. (1845). *The Holy Family*. Extracts in D. McLellan (Ed.), *Karl Marx: Selected Writings* (pp. 131–135). Oxford: Oxford University Press, 1977.

Marx, K., and Engels, F. (1846). *The German Ideology*. Moscow: Progress Publishers, 1976 edition.

Piaget J. (1970). *Genetic Epistemology*. London: Columbia University Press.

Sayer, D. (1983). *Marx's Method: Ideology, Science and Critique in "Capital"* (2nd edition). Brighton: Harvester.

4

Dialectical Conceptualization and Understanding Capitalism

Throughout this book, I am trying to persuade readers that it is possible for people to create an alternative vision of socialism, a humanized and democratized approach to the future, a vision that will enable us to engage in social and economic transformation. However, I also contend that this is only a possibility. We have to have the will or desire to enter into open and empathetic dialogue with one another to create a vision that can enlist commitment. Equally important, we have to develop a critical, a dialectical, understanding of our present conditions. In this chapter, I try to contribute to the second requirement by providing further discussion of Marx's dialectical understanding of capitalism and by relating to it to some of our contemporary experiences of living within capitalist societies. First, however, I go into greater detail about dialectical conceptualization because I am convinced that this more complex understanding is necessary to fully comprehend and appreciate Marx's explanation of capitalism. It also is necessary if we are to develop the ability to recognize and apply dialectical concepts.

At one time, I agreed with the many marxist scholars who were convinced that Marx had applied a dialectical *method* of analysis to his study of capitalism and its historical development. In philosophy—and many of those scholars were philosophers—"method" means a systematic, formal or abstract approach that is applied *a priori* to the content and is therefore divorced from a particular content and equally applicable to all content. I did not ignore, but certainly misinterpreted, Marx's protestation that the form of enquiry must differ from the form of presentation. Therefore, I must offer a rather long quotation from Marx's "Postface" in 1873 to the second edition of Volume 1 of *Capital*. This is actually a warning to those who then were and since have been trying to formalize his method of inquiry on the basis of his presentation. After Marx quoted in detail a review of Volume 1, he posed a question but then went on to issue the warning.

> But what else is he [the reviewer] depicting but the dialectical method?
>
> Of course the method of presentation must differ in form from that of inquiry. The latter has to appropriate the material in detail, to analyse its different forms of development and to track down their inner connection. Only after this work has been done can the real movement be appropriately presented. If this is done successfully, if the life of the subject-matter is now reflected back in the ideas, then it can appear as if we have before us an *a priori* construction.
>
> My dialectical method is, in its foundations, not only different from the Hegelian, but exactly opposite to it. For Hegel, the process of thinking, which he even transforms into an independent subject, under the name of "the Idea", is the creator of the real world, and the real world is only the external appearance of the idea. With me the reverse is true: the ideal is nothing but the material world reflected in the mind of man, and translated into forms of thought. [Marx, 1873, p. 102]

Although Marx did not apply a formal dialectical method to his study of economic history, he did "track down . . . inner connections," dialectical contradictions within history. When he refers to his "dialectical method," this must refer to his dialectical presentation of the historical development of capitalism in his economic writings. Nevertheless, and this is crucial to the points I made in the opening paragraph of this chapter, he had to have an orientation or mode of conceptualizing that enabled him to recognize and "track down" the dialectical contradictions that could explain the detail of his historical research. Given his intellectual formation within a Hegelian tradition, he could not have escaped such an orientation toward dialectical conceptualization, but he could develop and transform it.

In chapter 3, I offered a definition of a dialectical contradiction. I drew this definition from a section of Marx and Engels' 1845 text, *The Holy Family*, a section that Marx wrote, and I begin my fuller elaboration of Marx's dialectical conceptualization by repeating the definition but in terms of a manner of conceptualizing. Dialectical conceptualizing involves apprehending a real phenomenon as either part of or the result of a relation, a unity of two opposites that could not have historically developed nor exist as they presently do outside the way in which they are related. In more general terms, thinking or conceptualizing dialectically entails thinking in terms of relations. However, this is a very distinctive and precise manner of thinking about relations, one that I now explain.

In the quotation above, Marx used several terms in a precise manner, but one in particular is very important to this explanation. He referred to "*inner*," not "inter," connections. The choice of using one of these terms rather than the other signals the difference between conceptualizing relations internally as opposed to externally. I will draw on an article by Charles Tolman (1981) to explain the difference.[1]

Both historically and currently, a great deal of academic analysis and theorizing entails ordering the plethora of natural and social phenomena by placing them into categories. Membership in a category depends on members sharing certain key attributes that distinguish them from members of other categories. In many areas of study this type of categorical thinking has led and continues to lead to advances in knowledge (e.g. the natural science categorization of the plant and animal species). Nevertheless, the more people make sense of their world through categorization, the more some people are pushed to the realization that further understanding will only come from the recognition of the way in which the members of separate categories are related in the real world (e.g. once again, plants and animals). Relational thinking does not replace categorical thinking, but it does open up the possibility of the development of more complex and accurate understandings.

However, there are two very different and distinctive ways of thinking about relations. As mentioned above, we can understand relations or the nature of a relation as either external or, alternatively, internal. Marx's explanation of capitalism primarily involves a form of conceptualization based on internal relations; therefore, it is important to discuss the difference between external and internal relations.

To conceptualize relations externally involves apprehending the *interaction* of two existing categories—for example, human beings and some other category of the natural or social world. The already existing attributes of one category interact with the already existing attributes of the other and, in so doing, and for better or worse, produce something new, which is often referred to as a synthesis. The attributes of the categories that are in relation or interaction do not change but may produce a result, even a new category, that is a synthesis of the existing attributes. If you are good at visualizing explanations, think about the overlapping circles in a mathematical Venn diagram. The relation, or interaction, is depicted by the overlap of the circles. The person who is conceptualizing in terms of external relations focuses on the outcome of the interaction. This form of conceptualizing has led and will continue to lead to many advances in knowledge and understanding (e.g. the effects of human behavior on the natural environment).

Nevertheless, there is a different manner of relational thinking which leads to even more complex and accurate understandings. This is the type of dialectical conceptualization employed by Marx in his explanation of capitalism. It is based on understanding the internal nature of the relations between entities—that is, the real phenomena of the world that are reflected in our mental categories. Instead of just recognizing that entities interact, thinking in terms of internal relations involves focusing on the relation and observing or studying the way in which it regulates the development, the shaping and reshaping, of the attributes of the related entities. This is, inherently, a very historical mode of conceptualizing and understanding: the relation or its nature endures, but, throughout history, it serves to determine the further progressive or regressive development of the entities in the relation, the unity of opposites I referred to earlier. This should become much clearer later when I discuss Marx's explanation of the labor–capital relation and his dialectical concept of class.

Marx's concern was to explain to us the antagonistic, dialectical contradictions, relations, of capitalism. By conceptualizing and presenting these as internal relations, Marx was able to dispel the notion that such antagonisms could be resolved through reforms. He maintained that in such relations one of the opposites depended, for its continuous existence, on a position of advantage—on preserving the relation. It was the "positive" because it had to develop in ways that would positively preserve the relation. For example, capital is the "positive" in its relation to labor. The other opposite, labor in this example, is the "negative," or potential "negative," because it is in its interest to abolish or negate, not reform, the relation. By doing so the negative opposite abolishes itself as a separate and subordinate entity, or group in the case of the working class. Of course, the people are not abolished. Human beings divided by class, or by any relations of domination and oppression, become or create the conditions to become Humanity—that is, people united by common interests, values and goals that could create social justice. Marx's proposal for human action to begin the creation of a truly "human history" is referred to as the "negation of the negation." In less philosophical terms, labor (the potential negative) can liberate itself from domination and exploitation only by abolishing the relation that constitutes the members of this class in a negative position—by abolishing class and all other relations of domination (Marx,[2] in Marx and Engels, 1845, pp. 35–37).

USING CONCEPTS MORE FLUIDLY

I promised in chapter 3 to return to the point about our need to use concepts more fluidly—more dialectically—because we will need to do so to engage in authentic local and global social transformation.

My primary intent in chapter 3 was to explain Marx's distinctive theory of consciousness—in fact, a theory of praxis—that was revolutionary because it established the dialectical unity between our sensual experience of life and our thinking or consciousness. This revolutionary theory of conscious thought underpinned Marx's manner of explanation and is always my point of departure for interpreting him. To explain some of the earliest ways in which he used and attempted to portray his dialectical conceptualization, I draw on two concepts (already mentioned in chapter 3) that have attracted the attention of many marxist scholars: the concepts of alienation and ideology. Unfortunately, most books and articles deal exclusively with one or the other of these concepts rather than the relation between them. My contention is that all of Marx's important concepts express and depict an inseparable, a dialectical, unity or relation.

When Marx wants us to consider the active, sensual experience within which people develop the fragmented, distorted form of consciousness that he critically terms ideology, he beckons us to that consideration with an analysis of the humanly produced process of alienation. This analysis focuses on the way in which human beings, within capitalist social relations, produce the tangible products of the material world. His concept of alienation depicts a process by which the results of human labor are not conceived, by those who produce them, prior to their production and, once produced, have nothing to do with the actual people who have labored to make them. Furthermore, the objects, the wealth, they create are an externalization of their "inner life," their skills, capacities, knowledge and creativity, and these "powers" once externalized in alien objects become a force that dominates them (Marx, 1844, pp. 78–79). In Marx's time, the vast majority of human labor subject to capitalist social relations served to produce tangible agricultural or manufactured commodities. His explanations of alienation, as a consequence, at least in his early writings, utilize examples from these areas of human labor. However in his later writings (see the appendix to *Capital*, Volume 1, "*Resultate*": Marx, 1866), he discusses and asks us to understand that many other forms of human labor will eventually be reconstituted within the alienating labor–capital relation. These include all sorts of labor that we think of as immune from, perhaps above, the profit motive, such as educational and intellectual endeavors. I go into more detail about this later. For the moment, it is important to note that the transition from creative work to alienating labor is a historical process, sometimes a quite lengthy one. Even in agriculture and manufacture, the transition did not happen over night. Historical studies offer many examples of the ways in which working people attempted to struggle against or resist being drawn into the exploitative and alienating relations of capitalism (see Novak, 1988; Thompson, 1974). However, then, as perhaps now, they had no concept with which they could name the real oppressor—the relation that was the source of their alienation.

I need to return to one of the main reasons why Marx used this concept of alienation. When he employed it, he described active, sensuous human experience, people's engagement in the production and reproduction of the experience of alienation. In our own times, some academics use the term "alienation" to refer to a pathological or nearly pathological psychological state of mind. Marx never would have attributed and reduced what had become a fairly normal feature of human consciousness to a pathology of individual origin and maladaptation. When Marx wanted us to consider the influence of alienating labor and existence on our consciousness, he urged us to consider another concept, viz. ideology, and its most extreme manifestation, the "commodity fetish."

As I said in chapter 3, in the 1840s Marx used this concept of ideology to refer to a mode of thinking, whether common sense or academic, that was partial and fragmented. As a consequence, it produced a distorted understanding of the real world. Ideological consciousness was not false, in the usual sense of the word, but it was distorted and therefore a barrier to understanding the actual nature of reality. Even though in his later, economic texts he does not use the actual term "ideology" a great deal, the sense of the term—his conceptualization of ideology—is of fundamental importance to his critique of capitalism and the manner of thinking related to it. To reiterate some points I made earlier: in Volume 1 of *Capital*, where Marx explains the development of the commodity form of a product of human labor, especially the mature stage of this development within the labor–capital relation, he also explains the consequent effect on our consciousness. We tend to think that the value of a commodity derives from some property inherent in it, rather than understanding that the value is constituted within the labor–capital relation and that the magnitude depends upon the degree to which or intensity with which the relation is exploitative. He refers to the form of this ideological consciousness as the "commodity fetish," wherein we come to desire, even lust after, commodities because we associate their values with their intrinsic properties. We conceptualize a relation between things, rather than the actual social relations, class relations, within which value is constituted. With each concept, whether alienation, ideology or the commodity fetish, he beckons us to consider different aspects of a total dialectical process, a historical process the development of which Marx depicted through the *inner-action* of opposites—dialectical contradictions.

One of the best examples of Marx's dialectical conceptualization and consequently of his more fluid use of concept was his concept of class and, accordingly, the definition of class that can be derived from the concept. It is worth mentioning that many academics, both marxists and nonmarxists, have either agonized over or criticized his "failure" to leave us a clear definition of class. It also is important to remember that many political activists, left and right, have held rigidly to a static concept of the working class, viz. usually male manufacturing labor. With the numerical decline of workers employed in manufacturing labor, in various nation states some commentators have become mesmerized by ideological notions such as "the demise of the working class" or the idea that we have entered the ultimate "progressive" era of a classless society. Marx's dialectical conceptualization of class demonstrates how ridiculous such thinking about our current conditions is. He also challenges a great deal of contemporary political activity and analysis from the left, which attempts to marginalize or exclude class as a fundamental aspect of social division and injustice.

Marx's concept of class is a historical/dialectical one. Inclusion within his concept of class was not based on what commodity a person produced, how much people were paid for their labor or their consciousness of their class position. It was based on another criterion of production, viz. the production of surplus value, the basis of capitalist profit, accumulation and continuing development. In the "*Resultate*" (Marx, 1866), Marx refers to the producers of surplus value as "productive workers." In this appendix, we can find his most systematic and elaborate dialectical conceptualization of class. I will try to offer you the definition of class that can be culled from this valuable and very extensive source.

When Marx wanted to encapsulate the present and potential membership of the working class, he tended to use the term "proletariat." The term referred to all those who were employed in the production of surplus value; in his time, this included men, women and children engaged in most forms of industrial and even some aspects of agricultural production. However, the term also included those who were employed but who, as yet, did not produce surplus value but who could if their work was reconstituted within the labor–capital social relations of production (e.g. service-sector workers, even teachers and artists). In addition, it also included the unemployed, the reserve "army of labour." This term, the proletariat, signals a historical concept of class which should encourage us to consider and relate to not only present but potential allies.

There were also times when Marx needed to focus his analysis more precisely on the current producers of surplus value, and when this was necessary he used the term "productive labor," the current producers of surplus value, not a particular commodity. Yet again when he needed to establish the very special commodity that laborers sell to capital, he refers to *labor power*—not just labor. The term "labor power" indicates that this commodity, purchased for a wage, has a variable use-value that can be expanded within the social relations of production through various methods of exploitation—extended considerably beyond any equity with the wage, or exchange-value, that purchases it. Marx was not changing his mind about his concept of class when he used these different terms. He was explaining his concept of class dialectically, reestablishing in each instance the aspect of the relation which would enable us to understand the process of working-class formation and the specific feature of capitalism he was explaining. Perhaps we should think of all these terms as subconcepts of Marx's dialectical concept of class—that is, working class. They share the common attribute or characteristic of referring to people with the present and/or future potential of producing surplus value that accrues to the capitalist class.

In this current conjuncture of capitalist history, wider share ownership and mass membership in pension schemes may lead readers to think that Marx's dialectical concept of class is no longer viable. Many people seem to think that these changes mean that all working people have a greater interest and investment in retaining the capitalist system; to some degree, the argument goes, we have all become capitalists. However, they ignore how marginalized and dispersed this semblance of ownership is. They forget that the goal was for humankind to come together to decide democratically and rationally what to produce and how to justly distribute the results on the basis of human need. Unfortunately, these forms of ideological thinking are symptomatic of the variants of socialism that have lost their way by focusing exclusively on the ownership of the means of production—capital—while ignoring the social relations of production. Surely historical research provides abundant evidence that cooperative ownership, nationalized ownership, even socialist state ownership continue to reproduce the same exploitative social relations of production characteristic of capitalism when production has to be geared toward the creation of value and subjected to the competitive forces of local, national and global markets. If we focus on, or hold on to, the social relations of production, Marx's dialectical concept of class retains its explanatory power. It also demonstrates to us how we can learn to conceptualize in a fluid, historical, dialectical manner that will enhance the complexity of our understanding and the consequent effectiveness of the decisions and actions we take to promote social transformation at all levels of our existence.

THE BASICS FOR A CRITICAL UNDERSTANDING OF CAPITALISM

Marx left us with a very complex and comprehensive depiction of capitalism. He explained the dialectical relations that serve to constitute it as a distinctive social and economic formation and that regulate its further development and the cyclical adaptations that capitalists have to make in the face of crisis. To realize the richness of this legacy, many people involved in social transformation for justice will need to engage in a serious reading and study of his texts. However, many other people who must be involved will have no time for this in our present conditions of existence. Nevertheless, I firmly believe—in fact, I know—that there are certain basic understandings that once grasped dialectically will render transformative action more effective and authentic. These are not difficult ideas but ones that to our peril have often been neglected or dealt with separately by those with the luxury of studying Marx in depth. In this section, my intent is to bring these ideas together. Some of Marx's most important ideas about the essence of capitalism were discussed in chapter 3, and these are fundamental to a basic understanding of capitalism; however, since readers will need to share them coherently and systematically with others, I shall summarize and risk a bit of repetition. I also offer further detail or elaborations and relate the ideas to some of the contemporary experiences of capitalism.

The Commodity Form → Labor Becoming a Commodity → and the Creation of Surplus Value

In chapter 3, I discussed Marx's explanation of the historical development of the commodity form. It is important to note that the full development of the commodity form and, for that matter, Marx's Labor Theory of Value—that is, value being created by labor time expended in production—only come into their own within capitalist relations of production. However, to explain the concepts with which we can grasp the essence of capitalism, Marx takes us step by step through the unfolding—the development—of the commodity form. He distinguished between the creations of human labor that he called products and those that had developed into commodities. Products, once they were produced in surplus to the requirements of the producer, could be traded for others on the basis of need or some overt form of social convention. However, once the same results of human labor develop into the commodity form, they acquire two values. They continue to have a use-value that pertains to some historically and culturally specific requirement for satisfying human need; however, they can be acquired only by those who can accommodate their second value, the exchange-value, which is a fundamental factor in determining price. Human need as the basis for exchange is no longer fundamental. Purchasing power, the power to buy, becomes the fundamental criterion for determining whether or not human needs will be met.

Sometimes the results of human labor can assume the commodity form for a considerable period of time without being problematical in terms of not being available to meet all humans' needs. For example, in our own lifetime and before, education developed into the commodity form. However, in places where it increasingly became a universal provision, the local or national state rather than private individuals often met the exchange-value. Nevertheless, once products or services acquire this form, the labor that produces them can be incorporated more easily within the exploitative, dehumanizing social relations of capitalism. This is exactly what happened when manufacturing and agricultural labor developed into the commodity form. Workers could create useful products only when and if they worked for a wage paid by their employers. However, their subsumption within the actual labor–capital relation that is productive of surplus value can entail even more time and often struggle and resistance from the people who can "feel" themselves being drawn into a relation of exploitation. The main point is that this further transition cannot take place unless the results of human labor have acquired the commodity form.

In our present stage of capitalist development, there are many examples of this process taking place. The ones with which I am most familiar pertain to various areas of postcompulsory education. The learning colleagues (mature students) with whom I work come from many different arenas of postcompulsory education—for example, literacy and basic education, extramural education, trade union education, community education and development and further and higher education. The vast majority of these people complain about the "stress" they suffer from all sorts of pressure, especially those arising from having to expand their own work loads in recording and monitoring their performance or covering the work of former colleagues who have left or been made redundant. Many feel that they are no longer educationalists—professional educators—but technicians whose intellectual and creative skills have been incorporated in learning packages the consumption of which they now only disseminate, manage and assess. Their future employment, which they feel very anxious about, depends on the productivity or efficiency they demonstrate in engaging in this process. Some refer to it as the deintellectualization of their work. If we understand that skill in all areas of work is a social not just a technical concept that involves power, control and creativity, what these people are describing is exactly parallel to the long recorded process of deskilling in industrial and agricultural labor—a process that facilitates the ability of capital to exploit or increase the exploitation of working people.

Most often, they refer to this experience as "stress." This is a convenient concept for the dominant bourgeois ideology because it serves to relate the cause of an actual state of human subjective experience to a pathological origin that lies within the individual's failure to adapt, a failure that can be ameliorated only by prescription drugs or counseling. I suggest an alternative concept of stress, at least with reference to the experiences I have mentioned, and by no means does it diminish the devastating effect that stress has on individuals. Contemporary, work-related stress reflects the experience of a transition from what was once a meaningful and creative area of human labor into one that is mechanical and potentially totally alienating and exploitative. Those of us who are working for social transformation need to be in touch with our own and other people's anxieties, but to engage in much more than palliative action we also need to use a dialectical comprehension of what is happening.

I am not suggesting that most educationalists have become part of a fully fledged labor–capital relation—only that we, and especially the next generation of educators, are being prepared to accept the total transition when it comes. No one in particular is preparing us, but there is a certain, very rational, logic that must prevail once the commodities of our labor become subject to market forces. Many of us have had to accept already that what we do must be cost-effective or self-financing. With further pressure on this basis in terms of determining what we do and how we do it, including the time it takes us to do it, there is not a great distance to travel—before our educational endeavors are recast within the labor–capital relation and the production of surplus value—before we become privatized, for example, and help to create educational establishments that expand and diversify through the process of capital accumulation (M becoming M′). It is already happening on a relatively small scale.

The point to remember, however, is that human labor must be purchased as a commodity, it must assume the commodity form before it can be reconstituted or subsumed within the labor–capital social relations of production and therefore capable of producing surplus value. Even before this, of course, the products of human labor must have assumed the commodity form.

The Social Relations and Social Forces of Production

It can appear that in using these terms Marx used two quite separate and therefore distinguishable concepts. I explained that the social relations of capitalist production are an internal relation that retains its basic exploitative features but which, in so doing, continuously reconstitutes class composition by incorporating an ever-wider range of human labor into the production of surplus value. Within this social relation—the labor–capital relation—labor also continuously constitutes most of the social forces of production. Because Marx often referred to the social forces of production by means of specific examples, many marxists have assumed that this concept referred to only the technical or nonhuman forms of capital—that is, capital accumulation (e.g. plant, machinery and sometimes organizational systems). Marx's concept was much more fluid and dialectical than this. He used it to refer to anything that contributed to or could increase the total productivity of a society at any historically specific point in time. Therefore, even developments in ideological emphasis, such as the current glorifications of the benefits of the "free market," can become social forces of production when they encourage human attitudinal changes that serve to increase productivity (Marx and Engels, 1846).

However, we also need to consider another very important factor which throughout capitalist history frequently becomes a social force of production. The social relations of production, the human factor, always have been and will continue to be potential social forces of production (p. 49).[3] Here we are simply considering another aspect of the dialectical relation between labor and capital. The social relations of production and the social forces of production are a unity of opposites, reciprocally determining one another, but at certain times the social relations move into and form an identity with the social forces—they become one—and increase the overall productive output (Marx, 1867, p. 451). In so doing the surplus value produced is increased. Marx's historical research revealed two different and general ways in which capitalists' enterprises made labor produce surplus value. One of these he referred to as the extraction of "absolute surplus value," and the other he termed "relative surplus value." Many readers will recognize something similar to if not the actual experience of one or both of these.

Absolute surplus value is extracted from labor by extending the length of the working day. In the past, before legislation protected some workers from the extremes of this practice, absolute surplus value was extracted by extending the length of working time by some duration that was in surplus to the time required to recoup the workers' wages—the exchange-value of labor power (pp. 283–426). The surplus, in excess of these costs, accrued to the capitalist firm and became the basis of profit and capital accumulation. Historically, union struggles have often been pitched against this form of exploitation. In our current circumstances, with the much more widespread experiences of part-time work, this form of surplus-value extraction is on the increase. (Try to keep in mind always that value is based on *labor-time* and that surplus value is unpaid *labor-time*.) It has been made easier for the exploiters because the majority of part-time workers, so far, are women who often are grateful to get back into or to enter the labor market and who often find part-time employment more conducive to fitting around their unpaid domestic work. Increasing numbers of men are also accepting part-time work or various part-time jobs because they are desperate to be employed. Whatever the situation, part-time workers are inculcated with the idea that their future employability depends on an attitude or eagerness to work until the job is done, or nearly done, for the day, and an acceptance of the futility in claiming overtime pay or expressing any form of resistance.

Marx distinguished between the two types of surplus-value extraction at a point in history when benevolent and socially concerned middle-class people were pressing for legislation to limit the legal length of the working day. He knew that capitalists would adapt to survive these legal restrictions. He knew because his historical research had revealed the emergence already of another form of surplus-value extraction which he predicted would become the dominant form for a considerable period of time. He referred to the result of this form of exploitation as "relative surplus value" (pp. 429–639). Relative surplus value is obtained by increasing the ratio between paid and unpaid labor in favor of the latter—for example, by intensifying the labor process (i.e., the productive labor of each worker) within a specified period of time.[4] Through history, and sometimes side by side, various methods have been and continue to be used to extract relative surplus value. These include technological advances that increase the productivity of each worker; organizational alterations in the actual labor process such as assembly lines and, more recently, quality circles that accomplish the same ends; and managerial strategies and the development of new corporate forms such as multinational and transnational firms. Marx did not think that one form of surplus-value extraction totally replaced the other; however, he did think that most capitalists would attempt to increase absolute surplus-value extraction before resorting to the necessary investment required for the extraction of relative surplus value. We need to understand how these two forms, perhaps both, are affecting working lives in this present conjuncture of capitalist history which is characterized by global competition for both markets and the finite amount of financial capital that can be invested profitably.

The need to increase labor productivity, by whatever means, within the competitive conditions of capitalism continuously creates one of capitalism's most insidious and antagonistic paradoxes. Although the process can produce an expanding work force in times of economic growth, existing markets of effective demand—that is, people who have the ability to purchase—soon become saturated. Commodities cannot be sold, and workers eventually join the ranks of the unemployed. However, since it is human labor that produces the surplus value that forms the basis of capitalist profit, this is also a crisis for capitalism. Therefore, those people who remain in employment, or more precisely within the subordinate position of the labor–capital relation, must be exploited either more extensively or more intensively, or both. Furthermore, because the growth and continuation of capitalism depends upon the total amount of surplus value produced by all capitalist firms (Marx, 1865), the capitalist social relations of production must be expanded into alternative areas of human labor and also exported throughout the world so as to create not only new markets but new human sources of surplus value.

Because these processes are inherent in the development of capitalism or can be understood as such with dialectical conceptualization, Marx was able to explain them more than a century ago. He explained how the social relations of production would become fetters on the further development of the social forces of production. In particular historical situations, the social relations cease being social forces of production and move into dialectical opposition with them (Marx, 1865,

p. 359; Marx, 1867, pp. 927–929; Marx and Engels, 1846, pp. 91–98). It is important to realize and always remember that capitalist production takes place to create value and ultimately profit, not material wealth (i.e., products and services) that could be enjoyed by all human beings. I assume that Marx never underestimated the ability of capitalists to adapt, and I think that he was trying to help the working class to understand that capitalism develops through crisis and adaptations to the same. Crisis after crisis has occurred, however, without the exploited engaging in a critical challenge. To our peril, we have ignored Marx's explanation.

We are in the midst of another crisis, perhaps the most expansive and devastating ever experienced by humankind. Can we learn this time, or will we just go on reproducing, on an ever-expanding scale, the dehumanizing effects of existing within what has become a global capitalist social formation?

Capitalism and the Response to Crisis

Marx's polemical writings, which were aimed at raising the consciousness and rallying the support of the working class, encouraged many marxists to assume that capitalism would collapse eventually due to its inherent tendency toward recurrent economic crisis. One of these would spell its "inevitable" demise. This assumption is an unfortunate legacy of Marx but one for which those who adhered to the assumption must bear some responsibility. Even Marx's polemical writings can be interpreted differently if read alongside and with a dialectical conceptualization of his more analytical or scientific texts. Nevertheless, I think it is fairly easy to understand why the collapse theory of crisis has been so persistent.

When, as currently, people experience some degree of capitalist crisis in the form of recessions or depressions, the activists of the left can be seduced into thinking that this is the final one, the one that will herald the collapse of the entire system. However, the seduction is only effective when they also assume that socialism is the natural and inevitable successor of capitalism and when they forget, or never knew, that Marx's explanation also implies that some even more diabolical arrangement (e.g. modern barbarism) equally contends for the historical role of successor. Even though I have mentioned some of these explanations earlier, I think that it is important to go into more detail about them and others at this point.

To understand why economic crisis is an inherent feature of capitalism, we need to hold on to other, related dialectical understandings. We also need these to understand the ways in which capitalism will adapt. First, the production of any commodity, with whatever use-value, will only occur if that production results in a profit that accrues to the firm that produces it. No matter how much surplus value is incorporated in the commodity, it must be sold for the goal of capitalist production to be achieved. Furthermore, for any capitalist firm to survive, it must produce a rate of profit that is competitive in terms of the profits produced by its national and international rivals. Competition, which is another inherent and necessary feature of the system, creates an average rate of profit. No firm can make a profit below this average, for other than a very short period of time, if it is to be successful in attracting some portion of the capital available for profitable investment (Marx, 1865). Firms need this to set in motion the next cycle of production. Even this part of Marx's explanation, which is acknowledged by most bourgeois economists, demonstrates that capitalism is a system riddled with unnecessary tensions, tensions that can have devastating effects but could be overcome if we created a system in which our prime objective was to use our productive capacity and improvements in it to meet and enrich human needs.

If we delve a bit more deeply into Marx's explanation, the scenario we see played out under capitalist social relations becomes even grimmer. Despite market analyses, production decisions about the immediate future are primarily responses to "effective" demand and its volume in the previous cycle of production—as well as whether it created an average or above-average rate of profit. Investment will flow into the firms with the greatest success, and more of their commodities will be produced, creating a glut of these on the market in terms of consumers' (purchasers') needs. The result is the saturation of existing local, national or even global markets. Production must be cut back or totally scrapped by the least successful firms, or plant and machinery must be used to diversify into the production of new or altered commodities. Whatever process of adaptation is used, many working people suffer. As the system is "cleansed," some capitalists and their families lose their livelihoods, and, of course, some of the productive capacity already produced by human labor is lost. However, on a far larger scale, waged and some salaried workers join the ranks of the unemployed. In our present conditions, there is the possibility that all of these people may not constitute even a reserve army of labor that can be drawn into employment and then cast back into unemployment according to the changing needs of capitalist firms. They all—many of us, potentially—could become the permanently unemployed.

To some commentators on the left, this seems to offer the prospect of hope. André Gorz (1985) thinks that the state will have to offer a "social wage" so that the unemployed and unemployable can continue to consume; he has held on to his understanding of the dialectical relation between production and consumption. However, my observations of our current "postmodern" condition lead me to the conclusion that this hope for a "social wage" is based on a naivety that breeds a false confidence in the future.

At this conjuncture in capitalist development, one of the primary ways in which firms, especially multinational and transnational ones, are adapting is to create what I call multiheaded or ever-needy consumers who can back their demand with purchasing power. Most of these consumers reside in the "developed" world or in elite enclaves elsewhere. However, a variety of factors, not the least of which includes the globalization of media images, have held out the promise of this life style of consumption to many peoples in the underdeveloped and socialist countries. Many elements of past and present bourgeois ideological thought—for example, "the free market," competition and individual rights to join a meritocracy—have been embraced by far too many people. These people, and often their national leaders, have mistakenly equated the propensity to consume an ever-greater amount of commodities with a Western-style bourgeois "democracy" and " free markets." Those in socialist states seem to have forgotten, at least in the short term, the socialist values and their experiences of security in terms of employment, housing, education and health care. They also ignore that it was from those values and experiences that they were able to effectively challenge national states that were not delivering the promises of social justice and the enrichment of human needs and that were using undemocratic forms of governance and methods to suppress and eliminate resistance. They also fail to recognize that capitalism and democracy itself are undergoing a new and more global phase of crisis and critique.

Whatever the circumstances or exact historical detail, my point is that one of capitalism's responses to our present stage of crisis is to create new and multiple needs among those who have become or remain "effective" consumers. "Niche marketing," together with constant revolutions in consumer technology that seem to many people to render their current possessions obsolete, have been very effective maneuvers. Perhaps even more effective has been the relentless drive to draw more and more members of the world's population into the capitalist social relations of production and the related market relations of consumption. According to my analysis, these two sets of relations, over time, become inseparable.

Capitalism also continues to exist by other forms of adaptation. To consider these, it is important to note that the rate of surplus value depends on the ratio between paid and unpaid labor—that is, increasing the ratio in favor of the latter. The paid labor has to provide for sustaining and continuing—the reproduction of—the working class. Some of the ways of doing this have been social or political—for instance, when the reproduction of labor power is subsidized by the state. We must recognize that the variants of the "welfare state" were created at times of crisis, greatly reducing the cost for capital in maintaining or increasing the skills, education, health, reemployability of the labor force. Furthermore, bourgeois ideological thinking related to unpaid domestic labor has always provided inestimable savings for the capitalist class in reproducing the working class.

Technological innovations can also serve to increase the ratio between paid and unpaid labor. First, when these increase labor productivity, they can serve to reduce the cost of consumer goods and therefore reduce the reproduction cost of the working class. However, keeping in mind that Marx's theory of surplus value is based on his consideration of the ratio between paid and unpaid labor, and that human labor is the only source of surplus value, I must share one of my present concerns—only a speculation. Microchips are a new technological introduction, and it seems to me that they share certain common characteristics that Marx pointed out to argue that human labor was the only source of surplus value. When microchips are used in certain ways and since their replacement cost has fallen to a minimal level, I fear that a new adaptive strategy may be available for creating surplus value. According to Marx, human labor sets to work other forms of capital that have a value based on past labor time, but this is a fixed or constant value. Therefore, constant capital is not capable of producing new value. Exploitative measures are used to work what Marx calls variable capital to produce surplus value. Labor power, which is used to produce value, has to be purchased again each day, week or month. To my way of thinking, some of the uses of microchips are not so very different. They can set fixed or constant capital to work for a period of time, and some have become, or potentially will become, if necessary, cheaper to purchase every day, week or month than waged labor. The fear behind this speculation derives from a concern that massive numbers of people in our world may become superfluous to the needs of capitalism. I hope my speculation is wrong, but it is based on a dialectical understanding of Marx's explanation of surplus value, and I think that it needs to be investigated by others with much more technological and economical expertise than I have.

Whatever you think of that speculation, my main point is that capitalism will persist by means of multiple forms of adaptation, or what some commentators on the left call "restructuring." This will go on so long as critical action for social transformation, based on dialectical conceptualization, remains underdeveloped. However, since the task of creating that understanding can seem so daunting, I must conclude this part of the discussion with a consideration of the possibilities for and the role of reform in our past and present conditions.

The Limits of Reform

A sad conclusion arises from understanding Marx's dialectical explanation of capitalism. Over the medium and long-term course of history, the system cannot be reformed so as to produce a more just future for humankind. There are even cases when reforms bring no real advances in the short term. A better future for humanity and the environment depends on a critically conceived strategy for abolishing the antagonistic dialectical contradictions that underpin and sustain the development of the capitalist system. These are the source of the injustices that characterize this mode of social and economic organization.

This conclusion does not mean, however, that activists and advocates for social transformation should eschew efforts for reform. People, throughout our world, must survive in the best way possible the uncertainties and in many cases the daily struggles for existence that are created by the conditions of global capitalism. Reforms can help to a degree in some cases. However, the campaigns and struggles for reform offer possibilities of achieving something much more hopeful. These have always involved some degree of organization and usually some elements of education. Organization and education are necessary ingredients for achieving authentic social transformation. They will need to be more extensive, coordinated, democratic and critical than they often have been in the past. However, for this to happen, activists, especially leaders, must have a clear understanding of the capitalist reality they are seeking to reform and eventually transform. They need this understanding to create a more just and humane reality. It is an introduction to that understanding which I have been trying to offer. Our efforts can also be more effective if we remember Marx's point about the negation of the negation—that the negative is only *potentially* negative. We need to consider how we might enable the "restless" negatives to realize their potential through critical/revolutionary praxis. I discuss this in chapter 5.

Marx was very clear in depicting the devastations created by capitalism, but he also stressed that the system had increased human productivity and that we need an increased level of productivity in order to establish a form of human organization based on meeting human need rather than the creation and accumulation of profit and capital. Therefore, our visions for the future must be based, to a degree, on a clear and critical analysis of our material world and astute decisions about what can be preserved, although transformed, within alternative social relations. I must point out once again that Marx's vision of the future was not based on a leveled-down concept of basic needs like food and shelter. Of course, it included these but went far beyond them by being dialectical, developmental and culturally and historically specific.

If and when capitalism is abolished and people attempt to create a more just world, they will have to scrutinize the technology, science and other factors of productive capacity which have been developed within capitalist social relations. They will have to decide whether the factors that were developed primarily to serve the goal of profit maximization were developed in a manner that could be detrimental to humankind and the environment. Even when such conclusions are reached, I suspect that we could recast many of these intellectual achievements within a framework of altered goals and transformed social relations. In other words, humanity will not need to start from scratch. We will be starting from a material world that is already rich in potential. Furthermore, socialists currently involved in the development of technology could begin, even if in only small ways, to influence future developments and innovations.

I have been trying to explain that there are limits to reform but also suggesting that there are much more effective ways in which we could work within the campaigns and struggles for reform. Both to organize and to educate, we need to use the spaces created by people's desires for reform. Organization may arise locally in communities and neighborhoods, but when infused with a project of radical/critical education, it can present the potential for authentic alliances over regional, national and eventually global spaces. In struggles for reform, whether won or lost, people can learn a great deal about the limits of reform and can begin to understand the reasons why these limits exist. However, from the beginning, some of those involved must have the critical understandings that will enable them to pose crucial questions to the others at appropriate times. I am implying that these people must initiate and engage in quite different, totally transformed educational relations, and in the next chapter I deal with these in detail through the writings of Paulo Freire and Antonio Gramsci. These relations of education or this form of education cannot be delivered "to" people or "for" people but only established *with* them.

NOTES

1. See also B. Ollman (1976), *Alienation*, 2nd edition (Cambridge: Cambridge University Press). Tolman draws on Ollman, but I think that to those unaccustomed to philosophical discourse his explanation is clearer than Ollman's.
2. Attributed to Marx by the editors of the *Collected Works*.
3. Alternative source: D. McLellan (Ed.), *Karl Marx: Selected Writings* (Oxford: Oxford University Press, 1977), p. 166. Complementary reading: K. Marx, "Appendix: The Results of the Immediate Process of Production" [*Resultate*]. In *Capital*, Vol. 1, 1867 (Harmondsworth: Penguin, 1976), pp. 1052–1058.
4. Increasing the ration between paid and unpaid labor in favor of the latter can also be achieved by cheapening the value of the commodities that are necessary for the reproduction of labor power—thus creating a relative devaluation in labor power. Later in this chapter I discuss one way this can be done through state intervention.

REFERENCES

Gorz, A. (1985). *Paths to Paradise.* London: Pluto.
Marx, K. (1844). *Economic and Philosophical Manuscripts.* Extracts in D.

McLellan (Ed.), *Karl Marx: Selected Writings* (pp. 75–112). Oxford: Oxford University Press, 1977.

Marx, K. (1865). *Capital,* Vol. 3. Harmondsworth: Penguin, 1981.

Marx, K. (1866). "Appendix: The Results of the Immediate Process of Production" [*Resultate*]. In K. Marx, *Capital*, Vol. 1, 1867. Harmondsworth: Penguin, 1976.

Marx, K. (1867). *Capital,* Vol. 1. Harmondsworth: Penguin, 1976.

Marx. K. (1873). "Postface to the Second Edition." In K. Marx, *Capital*, Vol. 1, 1867. Harmondsworth: Penguin, 1976.

Marx, K., and Engels, F. (1845). *The Holy Family.* In *Karl Marx and Frederick Engels Collected Works: 1844–45, Vol. 4*, London: Lawrence and Wishart, 1975.

Marx, K., and Engels, F. (1846). *The German Ideology.* Moscow: Progress.

Novak, T. (1988). *Poverty and the State.* Milton Keynes: Open University Press.

Thompson, E. P. (1974). *The Making of the English Working Class.* Harmondsworth: Penguin.

Tolman, C. (1981). "The Metaphysics of Relations in Klaus Reigel's 'Dialectics' of Human Development." *Human Development*, *24*, 33–51.

5

Education and Social Transformation: The Ideas of Freire and Gramsci

I previously referred to the distinction between limited/reproductive praxis and critical/revolutionary praxis. The first is the norm. The second is necessary to radical, social transformation; however, since it goes against the grain of our present conditions, it must be infused, in all contexts, with an alternative educational approach, an approach that can be applied in informal or what may appear to be noneducational contexts and formal ones as well. The distinction between the two forms of praxis and the educational implications of each is based on Marx's revolutionary theory of consciousness, his theory of praxis. Since Paulo Freire's and Antonio Gramsci's ideas about education and political practice are based on Marx's theory of consciousness, I have chosen to present them in this chapter for your consideration.

As already indicated, I am not referring just to formal education. Education takes place in a variety of contexts, most of which have the potential to be transformed and eventually revolutionized. Therefore, I prefer to use Freire's term "cultural action" to embrace all of these. Freire's term utilizes an anthropological concept of culture that includes all products, ideas and practices of human beings, and therefore it provides a further link to Gramsci's most important ideas about education.

I must state a very important qualification regarding the role of education in radical social transformation. The relations of education promulgated by Freire and Gramsci, those explained here, must be the basic ingredients of any cultural action for transformation project; however, they only *prepare* people to engage in authentic social transformation. Without them it will not happen; but on their own—that is, education on its own—cannot lead immediately and directly to social transformation. Nor should it be expected to do this. I hope that this will become clearer through my discussion of Freire's and Gramsci's ideas.

Those who are engaged in or who want to engage in cultural action for social transformation should not expect or even desire a methodological blueprint for their practice. Tactics or methods that are aligned with an overall strategy must be worked out according to the specific context in which they are applied. Nevertheless, I think that there is a great deal that we can learn from the ideas of Freire and Gramsci. Their ideas offer us an approach or a philosophy for education for transformation, rather than a step-by-step method or handbook/manual. In this chapter, I explain this philosophical approach by drawing on many quotations, sometimes quite extensive, from their writings, so that you can judge the compatibility of their ideas and the degree to which they can inform our various areas of transformative praxis.

Before delving into their ideas, I must share a concern about how Freire and Gramsci have been interpreted by radical educators or critical pedagogues in the United Kingdom and, I suspect, fairly commonly elsewhere. Instead of learning from these two writers, many British educators seem to view their ideas as incompatible. Freire has come to be associated with process, or pedagogy, and Gramsci with knowledge, content and organization. In fact, a wider debate about emphasizing process rather than content, or vice versa, is rife throughout education in Britain. I contend that both the wider debate and its expression within radical adult education (or any other site of transformative praxis) exemplify the tendency of bourgeois, reproductive praxis to separate or dichotomize that which belongs together. In addition to the necessary dialectical unity between process and content, process contains a content of its own that can either complement or contradict the explicit content. Furthermore, any content or body of extant knowledge is the result of methodological or analytical processes that may work either dialectically or ideologically. Therefore, methodological processes must be considered critically alongside the content. I think that both Freire and Gramsci were aware of the relation between process and content and that their strategies for educational and political work derive from a concern for grasping this dialectical unity.

The ideas of Freire and Gramsci presented here are, of course, a selection. However, it is not an eclectic one. I have tried to identify what Gramsci calls the "guiding thread" in these authors' ideas and to indicate when there is overlap and compatibility. Of course, in the quotations I draw from their writings, you will notice differences in emphasis and language, but these are to be expected from two people whose work emanates from quite different social, cultural and historical circumstances—no matter how much they share a common theoretical and analytical base. When these differences can lead to quite divergent or incongruous interpretations or applications, I comment on these.

I begin this discussion with Freire and his ideas because that is where my own work for transformation began and remains most firmly rooted. Reading and studying Gramsci added precision and rigor to my application of Freire's ideas and also added to my growing concern about the need to align cultural action for transformation projects to a broader political and cultural movement.

PAULO FREIRE

Paulo Freire is a Brazilian and is best known for his work in and influence upon mass literacy campaigns first in Brazil, then in Chile and later in Guinea Bissau, Nicaragua and elsewhere. Even though Freire uses the broader terms "cultural action" and "cultural revolution," he is usually associated with education. As a consequence, it is easy to ignore that almost everything he has written also deals with the role of revolutionary leadership—the way in which socialist revolutionary leaders must work and learn *with* the people, as well as their organizational role. Even though I begin with some comments about his educational ideas, as far as possible I attempt to avoid any separation between education and political thought.[1]

On a series of audiotapes that Freire recorded while visiting Australia, he explains that his thinking about education began long before his doctoral studies or his work on mass literacy campaigns. It began when he was a young man who went to work with the rural and urban poor because of his Christian convictions. It was the conditions of existence of the poor, and particularly the way they thought about these conditions, that led him to the writings of Marx and other marxists (Freire, 1974a). A learning group with which I was involved in the early 1980s first listened to those tapes at the same time that we were seriously studying Freire's writings in order to formulate our own radical approach to adult education. This was about two years before I undertook an in-depth and comprehensive study of Marx's writings and, therefore, before I understood either Marx's dialectical conceptualization or his theory of consciousness and negative concept of ideology. Therefore, in our learning group's initial encounter with Freire, I was unable to really fulfil my obligations and commitments as a radical educator or cultural activist for transformation because I did not understand how directly Freire's educational philosophy was based on Marx. In fact, Freire's writings assume of the reader a considerable grounding in Marx. This may be a fair assumption in Latin America but is clearly unfounded with reference to a North American or British readership, and this may go some way toward explaining why some of his ideas have been so readily incorporated by liberal/progressive educators.[2]

I cite here just a few examples of dialectical conceptualization that could be read as interesting metaphors in the absence of an understanding of Marx's dialectical thinking.

In discussing the oppressed (i.e. the subordinate opposite), Freire says:

> At this level, their perception of themselves as opposites of the oppressor does not yet signify involvement in a struggle to overcome the contradiction; the one pole aspires not to liberation but to identification with its opposite pole. [Freire, 1972, p. 22]

Even though the translator footnotes the word "contradiction" and explains that in the book it means "the dialectical conflict between opposing forces," it is not much help, unless one also knows that a dialectical contradiction is the unity of two opposites that could not exist as they are outside their relation to each other. One also misses the point that to liberate themselves the oppressed must engage in what Marx called "the negation of the negation" by negating their relation with the oppressor, thereby negating themselves as a separate and oppressed class or group. Freire continues:

> In this situation the oppressed cannot see the "new [person]" as the [person] to be born from the resolution of the contradiction, in the process of

oppression giving way to liberation. For them, the new [person] is themselves become oppressors. [pp. 22–23][3]

Drawing on Marx's dialectical theory of consciousness (i.e. the conception of consciousness as a dialectical unity between thought and action, praxis), Freire says:

World and [people] do not exist apart from each other, they exist in constant interaction. Marx does not espouse such a dichotomy, nor does any other critical, realistic thinker. What Marx criticized and scientifically destroyed was not subjectivity, but subjectivism and psychologism. Just as objective reality exists not by chance, but as a product of human action, so it is not transformed by chance. If [humans] produce social reality (which in the "inversion of the praxis" turns back on them and conditions them), then transforming that reality is an historical task, a task for [human beings]. [p. 27]

Of course, from this a reader can glean some idea about what Freire is implying. However, without Marx's detailed explanation of how a limited praxis—that is, one that, even when aimed at resistance, simply reproduces the given social relations or dialectical contradictions—produces the inversion and of how revolutionary or critical praxis must both critique the resulting ideological explanations and transform the relations that constitute the social contradictions, I am not sure how someone can put Freire's ideas into practice with any sort of precision. For readers well-grounded in Marx, Freire's writings can be read in a much more analytical and strategical way, and his analytical rather than merely philosophical debt to Marx becomes clear. With such a grounding, a much deeper meaning can be derived from the following quotation, where he is discussing a critical (dialectical) perception of reality developing amongst the oppressed:

This perception is necessary, but not a sufficient condition by itself for liberation. . . . Neither does the discovery by the oppressed that they stand in dialectical relationships as antithesis to the oppressor who could not exist without them . . . in itself constitute liberation. The oppressed can overcome the contradiction in which they are caught only when this perception enlists them in the struggle to free themselves. [p. 26]

"To free themselves" means, in terms of long-term strategy, to free themselves from the relation of the dialectical contradiction rather than to obtain only political freedom in the traditional democratic sense. Again with Marx as a background, Freire could not be clearer; but without that background, readers will take from Freire what seems meaningful to them. Furthermore, I know from my own experience that if you abstract Freire's ideas from their Marxist theoretical context, you will miss the precision of his analysis and ignore the revolutionary or transformative intent of his work.

One of Freire's most important contributions to education, or any form of cultural action for transformation, and to marxism itself stems from his understanding of Marx's theory of consciousness and his negative or critical concept of ideology in which "ideology," or "ideological," refers neither to a "system of beliefs" nor to "false consciousness" but to explanations, or actions and symbols based on such explanations, that are partial and fragmented and thereby distorted. Freire shares Marx's concern about how ideology, and what Freire also calls "a naive consciousness" (Freire, 1976,[4] p. 44), can serve to sustain an oppressive social formation. His educational projects are based on developing a critical (dialectical) perception of reality among the participants (Freire, 1972, pp. 15 fn., 26–29). He expects socialist cultural workers and revolutionary leaders to have already developed this perception. Their role, however, is not to tell the people what to think but to enable them also to think critically (pp. 99–101). His contribution (which I discuss in detail later) is an analysis of how to be *with* the people so that they can develop this way of thinking. Without it there will be no motivation for struggle and no authentic revolution. However, one of Freire's primary concerns is about how the ideology of the oppressors can continue to affect even those who have a critical perception of reality.

For Freire, as for Marx, ideology results from human beings' experiences within real relations or dialectical, social contradictions. Therefore, according to Freire, when revolutionary leaders communicate with the people, they must do so within relations that are the opposite of the oppressors' (p. 97). As indicated above, ideology is not just a matter of ideas or explanations but entails ways of relating and behaving. In the following quotation, he warns revolutionary leaders that they may be reflecting to the people a less than revolutionary option:

> I believe that one of the most difficult problems confronting a revolutionary party in the preparation of militant cadres consists in rising above the

canyon between the revolutionary option formulated verbally by the militants and the practice which is not always revolutionary. The petite bourgeois [liberal-democratic] ideology that permeated them in their class conditions interferes with what should be their revolutionary practice. . . . It's in this sense that methodological errors are always an expression of an ideological vision. . . . In so behaving, all they do is reproduce this dichotomy—typical of a class society—between teaching and learning. . . . They refuse to learn with the people. . . . Because of all of this I'm convinced that the effort to clarify the process of ideologizing must make up one of the introductory points in every seminar for preparing militants, simultaneously with the exercise of dialectical analysis of reality. [Freire, 1985, p. 163]

One of the most basic tenets of Freire's approach, then, is that cultural action for socialism is about developing a critical (dialectical) consciousness, a critical praxis, but this pertains as much to the leaders or educators as it does to the people, even if the former have a "theoretical," conceptual and analytical head start (pp. 156–163).

From what has been said thus far—and I return to this in detail later—Freire understands revolution to be a process with an important and essential educational component (Freire, 1972, pp. 43, 106). However, he also understands education to be a thoroughly political process—not just his approach to education but all education and every aspect of it (p. 52; see also Freire, 1974a). For Freire, every educational or cultural process can be seen as one that either domesticates people or aims to contribute to their liberation, or, rather, to prepare them collectively to liberate themselves (Freire, 1985, pp. 101–104). Hopefully it is clear that, for Freire, liberation is not aimed at individuals but, of course, will have a profound effect on them. Freire offers a very persuasive argument that educators' claims to neutrality are an impossibility. If educators are not encouraging people to question (to see their reality as a problem), to challenge and to change their reality, then they must be enabling them to accept it, adapt to it and to engage in its reproduction, unless, of course, their approach enables those with whom they work to see the latter as a tactic linked to the former. Therefore, educators and all other cultural workers must make a political choice between domestication and liberation and, in making that choice, be clear about whose interests they are serving (pp. 101–104; see also Freire, 1974a).

Needless to say, those who have claimed that Freire's approach to education is nonprescriptive have, in certain ways, interpreted him incorrectly. At the level of prescription, which suggests what educators "ought" to do, he is unequivocal. This, in turn, links back to the essential prescription that he shared with—and probably came to through his readings of—Marx. Both of them think that it is our human vocation to become more fully human (Freire, 1972, pp. 20–21). In Marx's terms, this would mean being at one with our "species-being" or that which makes our species distinctive from others. According to this analysis of human ontology, human beings are alienated from their human potential. Marx and Freire urge human beings to engage in a revolutionary process that would deliver human history into "human hands,"—that is, making it the critical and creative product of all human beings. There is no doubt that this is prescriptive, but we should not forget that it is no more so than the laissez-faire "flip-side" prescription. The difference, therefore, is not one between prescription and nonprescription, but one between the ethical basis of the prescription. The idea of being more fully human is at the core of Freire's thought; therefore, we should examine this idea in more detail.

Freire stresses that both humanization and dehumanization are real possibilities, but only the former is the vocation of the human species. To exist humanly, or to engage in the process of humanization, we need not wait for a revolution. Even in the most limiting situations we can begin to perceive those limits, our reality, critically and engage in the struggle to transform our societies (Freire, 1972, pp. 72–73). For Freire, humanization is not some philosophical or utopian demand but a real, historical possibility. It is the dialectical opposite of dehumanization, and to date it is constantly negated by dehumanization, or exploitation and domination: "Yet it is affirmed by that very negation . . . by the yearning of the oppressed for freedom and justice"(p. 20). He continues, stressing that dehumanization is a concrete historical fact rather than the natural destiny of humankind:

Dehumanization, which marks not only those whose humanity has been stolen but also (though in a different way) those who have stolen it, is a *distortion* of the vocation of becoming more fully human. This distortion occurs within history; but it is not an historical vocation. Indeed, to accept dehumanization as an historical vocation would lead to either cynicism or total despair. The struggle for humanization, for the emancipation of labour [from its relation with capital], for the overcoming of alienation, for the affirmation of [humans] as persons would be meaningless. This struggle is possible only because dehumanization, although a concrete historical fact, is *not* a given destiny but the result of an unjust order that engenders the violence in the oppressors, which in turn dehumanizes the oppressed. [pp. 20–21]

A critical perception of reality enables people to know what needs changing, but it has two other very essential functions. This critical, dialectical, perception together with an engagement in creating our conditions of existence is what it means to be fully human, and it is the right of every person, not of some privileged few (p. 61). Furthermore, it is this perception of reality that creates the will or the motivation in people to risk themselves in revolutionary struggle.

A deepened consciousness of their situation leads [people] to apprehend that situation as an historical reality susceptible of transformation. Resignation gives way to a drive for transformation and inquiry, over which [people] feel themselves in control. If [people], as historical beings, necessarily engaged with other [people] in a movement of inquiry, did not control that movement, it would be (and is) a violation of [their] humanity. Any situation in which some [people] prevent others from engaging in the process of inquiry is one of violence. The means used are not important; to alienate [people] from their own decision-making is to change them into objects. [p. 58]

Once again he is not just commenting on the oppressors but cautioning revolutionary leaders about their relations with the people. This passage also indicates that Freire thinks dehumanization is widespread. It is not just the poor who are alienated from decision-making and critical thinking but the vast majority of people living in the world, regardless of their form of government. Related to this is Freire's distinction between "being in the world" and "being with the world" (Freire, 1985, pp. 67–71).

According to Freire, animals are "beings in the world"; they must respond and adapt to given conditions. People, too, can be "beings in the world" when they lack either a scientific understanding of the natural world or the necessary "scientific" (dialectical) understanding of their social formation. To be thoroughly, humanly "with the world" means that people would have developed a critical perception and would have taken collectively their environmental, social, political and economic destiny into their own hands. But even to begin that struggle is to become "beings with the world."

As mentioned earlier, Freire's most important contribution to marxist thought is his analysis of how radical educators and political activists can work *with* people to enable them to think critically or dialectically about their reality. Repeatedly he emphasizes that such a perception cannot be given to or imposed on people (Freire, 1972, pp. 97–101). This concern is firmly located in Freire's understandings of Marx's negative concept of ideology and dialectical conceptualization. For Freire, grasping the dialectical content of reality is the necessary precondition for the beginnings of a human history created by all human beings (pp. 84–87). In a section where he discusses the program content of education for liberation—"the 'universe of themes' in dialectical contradiction"—he says:

> In such a situation, myth creating irrationality [ideology] itself becomes a fundamental theme. Its opposing theme, the critical and dynamic view of the world, strives to unveil reality, unmask its mythicization and achieve the full realisation of the human task: the permanent transformation of reality in favour of the liberation of [human beings]. [p. 74]

In a later section, he refers to a particular myth and in so doing encapsulates his approach to being with the people:

> Scientific [dialectical] and humanist revolutionary leaders . . . cannot believe in the myth of the ignorance of the people. They do not have the right to doubt for a single moment that it is only a myth [an element of the oppressor's ideology]. . . . Although they may legitimately recognize themselves as having, due to their revolutionary consciousness, a level of revolutionary knowledge different from the level of empirical knowledge held by the people. . . . They cannot sloganize the people, but must enter into dialogue with them, so that the people's empirical knowledge of reality, nourished by the leaders' critical knowledge, gradually becomes transformed into knowledge of the *causes* [dialectical contradictions] of reality. [p. 104]

In the next section, I describe the principles and strategies that underpin this approach to working with people. However, before going on to those details, it is important to make two further points.

When Freire says that we do not have the right to think that others are ignorant, he is not saying that we simply accept their perceptions of reality. These perceptions must be re-presented as a problem, because they may be limited by naive fatalism, permeated by the dominant class's ideology or locked into a limited awareness of a singular form of oppression (pp. 80–83, 149–150). Freire's ideas have been enthusiastically embraced by a variety of reformist campaigns, and his concept of "conscientization" (the process of developing the critical/dialectical perception) is often equated with "consciousness raising." The following passages clearly challenge these reformist interpretations and will hopefully help to set the record straight for radicals who may have dismissed Freire more because of the practices that claim to be based on his ideas than because of what he actually says:

> human beings do not get beyond the concrete situation, the conditions in which they find themselves, only by their consciousness or their intentions, however good those intentions may be. . . . Praxis is not blind action. . . . It is action and reflection. . . . In this sense, subjectivism—throwing itself into simple verbal denunciation of social injustice . . . while still leaving intact the structure of society—is just as negative as . . . mistrusting a rigorous and permanent scientific [dialectical] analysis of objective reality. [Freire, 1985, pp. 154–155]

Concerning palliative solutions, he says:

> Manipulated by the ruling classes' myths, the dominated classes reflect a consciousness which is not properly their own. Hence their reformist tendencies. Permeated by the ruling class ideology, their aspirations to a large degree, do not correspond to their authentic being. These aspirations are superimposed by the most diversified means of social manipulation. [p. 159][5]

Freire's approach involves starting with "where people are" but moving with them to an increasingly critical consciousness. Such a consciousness would enable people to understand how their own experience of oppression (e.g. race, class, gender, etc.) is linked to a total structure of oppression and to redefine their aspirations accordingly.

Freire's Approach

Clearly, this approach is about working *with* people rather than working *for* them or *on* them, but we must consider now the transformations that are essential to establishing this relationship with others. In very general terms, Freire's approach involves challenging and transforming the relations that pertain in traditional (bourgeois) cultural practices. The immediate goal of these transformations is the conscientization I referred to earlier. Freire uses the Latin American equivalent of this term to embrace in one word his advocacy of the need for a critical dialectical perception of reality in unity with critical, transformative practice (1985, pp. 82–87). The term "conscientization" expresses the inseparable unity between critically acting to transform relations and the critical transformation of consciousness. In other words, it is only within the experience of struggling to transform relations and the experience of the transformations that our critical consciousness can fully develop.

To initiate a Freirean approach, then, involves a detailed analysis of the relations that will need to be transformed. Although these may vary considerably in different social and historical contexts, two relations in particular seem to be relevant within any formal or nonformal educational setting and have important implications for many other areas of cultural work. For readers who are familiar with Freire's work, the relation between teachers and learners will be well known, but I must argue that it is frequently misunderstood.

The discussion offered in chapter 3 of a dialectical analysis of bourgeois education[6] drew directly on Freire's ideas. I will recap some of the essential points. Teachers and learners are a unity of opposites, or, in other words, a dialectical contradiction. Each is what it is by virtue of its relation to the other. For Freire, this is an antagonistic contradiction that must be overcome. The teacher possesses "already existing knowledge" that learners need. An antagonism results because learners, due to their dependency, are subordinate and teachers, as a dialectical consequence, are dominant. Therefore, teachers and learners constitute different groups in which the processes of teaching and learning have become separated or dichotomized. Another consequence of this is that the "act of creating new knowledge" becomes totally separated from the "act of acquiring extant knowledge." All of these separations are antagonistic because they limit the learning and creative potential of both groups.

With Freire's approach, the idea is to conceive of teaching and learning as *two internally related processes within each person*. This is why he uses rather cumbersome terms such as *teacher-learners* and *learner-teachers* to express the necessary transformations. Teachers do not cease being teachers but cease being the exclusive or only teacher in the learning group. They will need to relinquish authoritarianism but not authority. He emphasizes that *teacher-learners* must have plans, projects and goals or an overall intent within which they work, including their own learning (Freire, 1972, 1974a). *Learner-teachers* likewise do not cease being learners but join together with teachers in a mutual process, a unity, of teaching and learning (1972, 1974a.). However, as simple and straightforward as this transformation may sound, it is extremely difficult. Teachers on their own cannot transform this relation. They can initiate the change by challenging learners to consider the limitations of existing relations, but it is only when the learners accept the challenge that the actual, collective struggle to transform the relations begins. It is the beginning of the struggle because to truly establish the unity between teaching and learning within each person, the transformation of yet another relation must be sought simultaneously.

It is impossible to effect the transformation of the teacher–learner relation authentically until both teachers and learners transform their relation to knowledge (1972, p. 53; 1974a). In other words, *being or relating differently is inextricably bound up with knowing differently.* Given Marx's theory of consciousness (praxis) and Freire's understanding and use of it, this should not be surprising. I only want to emphasize that both transformations must be struggled for simultaneously. The task is all the more difficult in bourgeois societies because our relations to knowledge and our concepts of knowledge, our epistemologies, are constituted within and penetrated by bourgeois ideology. Both Marx and Freire stress that certain residues of the capitalist social formation will linger even after a socialist revolution. Bourgeois epistemology is one such residue that, until it is challenged and transformed, will remain a barrier to the realization of socialism or any authentic transformation of our social reality (1972, p. 128). In this century, it has proven itself to be a very real and pervasive barrier.

Like everything else that, in fact, results from social relations, bourgeois knowledge is perceived as a "thing," a commodity. If we possess it, it affects who we are, our status and self-esteem, and if we do not possess it, there is an equal and opposite effect on who we are and how we think about ourselves. A transformed relation to knowledge involves constantly scrutinizing what we know and constantly testing its adequacy as a tool for illuminating our real conditions and informing our action. Knowledge, therefore, cannot be conceived as a static possession but only as a mediation or tool between people and the world which either helps or hinders a critical perception of reality. And this is also true for the knowledge that may have resulted from grasping the dialectical movements of reality at a particular point in time. In fact, it is because social reality moves and develops according to dialectical processes that knowledge cannot be perceived as static (pp. 146–147; Freire, 1985, pp. 87–90, 105–107).

In Freire's approach to education, knowledge—the expert's and our own—becomes an object to which we direct our critical thought. Since knowledge is used to deepen our understanding of the themes or issues that arise from our material conditions, it must be constantly tested, questioned or problematized. All sorts of knowledge—academic, radical critique, personal—are central to Freire's approach, but as something we use rather than simply acquire. *Therefore, any knowledge is a means by which we begin learning rather than an end in itself.* When knowledge enables us to unmask or "track down" the dialectical contradictions of our reality, it becomes the springboard for the creation of new knowledge or the deeper understanding of the world which we will need for developing a revolutionary transformative praxis. When, on the other hand, the critical scrutinizing of a form of knowledge reveals that it is concealing those contradictions, it can be used to inform us of ideological processes and results.

Some radical educators in Britain appear to have rejected Freire's ideas because they can see no space for a consideration of radical content. Nothing could be further from the case; however, perhaps the role of content or knowledge in Freire's approach is only clear given an understanding of Marx's negative concept of ideology and the epistemological and ontological shifts required by Freire's approach.

To effect the transformation of teacher–learner relations and relations to knowledge, Freire proposes that learning must take place within a revolutionary form of communication, viz. dialogue. He calls it, "the seal of the transformed relations," but it is also the process that enables these transformations to take place:

> Only dialogue, which requires critical thinking, is also capable of generating critical thinking. Without dialogue there is no [real] communication, and without communication there can be no true education. Education which is able to resolve the contradiction between teacher and student takes place in a situation in which both address their act of cognition [understanding] to the object by which they are mediated. [Freire, 1972, p. 65]

With reference to the last point and perhaps more clearly, elsewhere he says:

> While in education for domestication one cannot speak of a knowledge object but only of knowledge which is complete, which the educator possesses and transfers to the educatee; in education for liberation there is no complete knowledge possessed by the educator, but a knowable object which mediates educator and educatees as subjects in the knowing process. Dialogue is established as the seal of the epistemological relationships between subjects in the knowing process. [Freire, 1974b, pp. 20–21]

Dialogue is not achieved easily. It involves the struggle to transform the relations I have just discussed; therefore, it is a form of critical praxis (Freire, 1972, p. 99; see also Allman and Wallis, 1990). It is a form of communication that is appropriate for cultural action in any arena of radical transformative praxis (Freire, 1972, pp. 98–99).

In dialogue, teachers and learners learn to relate differently to each other by relating differently to knowledge, and vice versa. I can best explain dialogue and these different relations by contrasting it to two traditional forms of education communication, viz. lecture and discussion. On one of the tapes in the series mentioned earlier (Freire, 1974a), Freire tries to clarify his approach by contrasting it with what he calls "banking education." However, it becomes clear in his description of the banking teacher that what he is criticizing is not a method—the lecture—but the teacher's relation to knowledge, which affects how the method is used. The gist of what he says is that the teacher goes to her study or the library and researches the topic for the lecture. She prepares her notes and organizes the appropriate order of presentation, and in this process her "act of knowing" is completed. She has only now to transmit the results to the learners. Freire says that he is convinced of just the opposite: "For me to know, I need another subject of knowing. . . . Because of you [the other subject of knowing] I know that I can know more." I would argue that the same "banking" relations to knowledge pertain in most discussions as well as the vast majority of progressive pedagogy. For example, let us look at what takes place in a discussion.

People enter into discussion in order to articulate what they already know or think. If the discussion takes place in an educational context, the teacher will want to use the discussion method to be sure that the students have understood and can express or apply what they have

learned prior to the discussion. The discussion method also helps people to learn the skill of arguing their interpretation or their knowledge against that which is expressed by others. Discussion is an ordered and managed communication of monologues. If everyone in the group shares a similar understanding, discussion can be an extremely self-confirming or reassuring experience. However, often there is a fair amount of conflict and therefore competition among the monologues. As a consequence, there must be a discussion leader who can guarantee equal time and space to each participant. This leader should also be able to manage the dynamics of the group so as to contain conflict and assure the harmony and cohesion of the group. In an educational context, the leader (usually the teacher) should also acknowledge the correct understanding when it is voiced or re-pose the question to yet another participant when the previous one has either got it all wrong or at least not quite right. In other words, there is some knowledge that it is the objective to know and to correctly express and/or apply.

Dialogue, in contrast and complete opposition, involves the critical investigation of knowledge or thinking. Rather than focusing only on *what* we think, dialogue requires us to ask of ourselves and each other *why* we think what we do. In other words, it requires us to "problematize" knowledge (Freire, 1972, ch. 3). This means all sorts of knowledge—academic and personal knowledge—as well as how we have come to a subjective knowledge or "feeling" about some issue. All of these types of knowledge are susceptible to ideological contamination, and therefore they must be critically scrutinized by the learning group.

> By stimulating "perception of the previous perception" and "knowledge of previous knowledge", decoding [a process within dialogue] stimulates the appearance of a new perception and the development of new knowledge . . . potential [critical] consciousness supersedes real [limited] consciousness. [p. 87]

Since some of the knowledge under investigation will be central to the way in which individual participants think about themselves and their world, trust is essential to dialogue. However, real feelings of trust, among the members of a learning group, will not preexist the struggle to achieve dialogue. Trust is created within that struggle (p. 137). What does accelerate the achievement of dialogue is at least some level of commitment, among participants, to develop a deeper and more critical understanding of their reality. In dialogue, each participant helps the other, and all are helped to explore the historical and material origins of their thought. Dialogue, therefore, is a collaborative form of communication and learning which, even though it involves challenge, creates trust rather than animosity. Most fundamentally, it is a form of communication that enables people to dialectically conceptualize their reality.

The struggle to transform the antagonistic relations and to keep them transformed demands the constant unity of action and critical reflection. The unity of action and reflection in dialogue is a form of critical praxis just as it is in political action. We don't think, then act and turn off our critical reflection. Nor can we think critically without an active struggle to do so. Freire says:

> Let me emphasize that my defence of the praxis implies no dichotomy by which this praxis could be divided into a prior stage of reflection and a subsequent stage of action. Action and reflection occur simultaneously. . . . Critical reflection is also action. [p. 99]

Freire's *Pedagogy of the Oppressed* (1972) contains the most fully elaborated explication of his educational philosophy. However, what is often ignored is that this book is also about revolutionary strategy. Freire argues that revolution must entail two phases. One he calls "cultural action" and the other "cultural revolution."[7] Cultural action refers to any type of project that attempts to transform relations prior to the taking of power at the exact moment of political revolution. The aim of these projects is to enable people to develop a critical perception of their oppression and, as far as possible prior to the revolution, or social transformation, to prepare themselves for full active engagement in cultural revolution (pp. 30–31, 103–107). Cultural revolution is a permanent process in which conscientized people engage in the continuous creation and recreation of their society. Instead of taking place in opposition to the state, it is supported by the revolutionary state or whatever political organization replaces the bourgeois state (Freire, 1985, ch. 7).

At several points in his writing, Freire addresses the problem of revolutionary leaders or socialist educators who think that there is no possibility of education for liberation within capitalist state institutions. He says that many of them believe in dialogue with the people but think that it will only be possible after power has been wrested from the oppressors (Freire, 1972, p. 105). In answer to their doubt, he argues:

One aspect of the reply is to be found in the distinction between *systematic education* which can only be changed by political power, and *educational projects*, which should be carried out *with* the oppressed in the process of organizing them.

The pedagogy of the oppressed . . . has two distinct stages. In the first, the oppressed unveil the world of oppression and, through praxis, commit themselves to its transformation. In the second stage, in which the reality of oppression has been transformed, this pedagogy ceases to belong to the oppressed and becomes the pedagogy of all [people] in the process of permanent liberation. In both stages, it is always through action in depth that the culture of domination is culturally confronted. In the first stage, this confrontation occurs through the change in the way the oppressed perceive the world of oppression; in the second stage, through the expulsion of myths created and developed in the old order which, like spectres, haunt the new structure emerging from the revolutionary transformation. [pp. 30–31]

Again, speaking about revolutionary leaders, he says:

When they deny the possibility that leaders can behave in a critically educational fashion before taking power, they deny the revolution's educational quality as *cultural action* preparing to become *cultural revolution.* [p. 106]

One of the reasons why cultural revolution must continue after the decisive revolutionary moment was stated above, viz. to rid the new society of all of the ideological residue (Marx called it "muck") of the previous one (Marx and Engels, 1846, p. 60). Freire also stresses another reason. With science harnessed to meeting and enriching human needs, human beings will create more complex societies. Therefore, they must be critically vigilant regarding what they create so that technology is not allowed to replace human choice as the determining factor in human history (Freire, 1985, pp. 88–89).

Throughout his writings, Freire expresses his concern that we must guard against one form of oppression replacing another. This is why he urges revolutionary leaders to enter into the same types of relations with the people that he proposes for teachers and learners. Like the socialist educator, the political activist or any other cultural worker for social transformation must begin with people's understandings of the world but then reframe this perception as a problem. Re-posed as a problem, reality becomes the object of their critical inquiry:

Cultural synthesis . . . does not mean that the objectives of revolutionary action should be limited by the aspirations expressed in the world view of the people. If this were to happen (in the guise of respect for that view), the revolutionary leaders would be passively bound to that vision. Neither invasion by the leaders of the people's world view nor mere adaptation by the leaders to the (often naïve) aspirations of the people is acceptable . . . . Cultural synthesis serves the ends of organization; organization serves the ends of liberation . . . the oppressed, in order to become free, also need a theory of action. . . . Nor can the people—as long as they are crushed and oppressed, internalizing the image of the oppressor—construct by themselves the theory of their liberating action. Only in the encounter of the people with the revolutionary leaders . . . in their praxis—can this theory be built. [Freire, 1972, pp. 149–150]

Freire clearly sees the need for leaders, but leaders who work and learn with people rather than for them.

The leaders do bear the responsibility for co-ordination—and, at times, direction—but leaders who deny praxis to the oppressed thereby invalidate their own praxis. By imposing their word on others, they falsify that word and establish a contradiction [a formal logical rather than dialectical one] between their methods and their objectives. If they are truly committed to liberation, their action and reflection cannot proceed without the action and reflection of others.

Revolutionary praxis must stand opposed to the praxis of the dominant elite, for they are by nature antithetical. [p. 97]

With Freire, this is not just a matter of principles but a historical necessity. It is the only means by which we can make certain that one form of oppression is not simply replaced by another. His concern is related to his analysis of the "oppressor within" (pp. 23 ff.).

The oppressor within is the psychological result of the social relations between the oppressors and the oppressed. The oppressor's ideology—ways of thinking, motives and ways of behaving—actually penetrates the subjectivities of the oppressed. They have no other model, other than the oppressor, of what they might aspire to be. This can be true for their leaders as well. Therefore, Freire urges that the only way to counter this tendency is for socialist educators and revolutionaries—in every aspect of their "being"—to offer a model of the revolutionary option (pp. 104–107). To do this, and to sustain it, means that people who join the struggle for social transformation will have to understand the necessity for the continuous critical examination of the oppressor within themselves (pp. 36–37). This is especially important during the stage of cultural action when structural change has not yet occurred.

During cultural action projects, we can only ever experience the revolutionary option in an abbreviated form. But even that form should offer a clearer or more concrete idea of what we are seeking to become. It is crucial for prefigurative struggle to offer a "glimpse" of an authentic humanized, democratic, socialist alternative. People need to experience and feel the difference, rather than just hear or read about it, if their consciousness is to undergo an authentic change. Dialogue, as a form of education and political communication, is one example of what I mean by a "glimpse." It is an extremely important one, because it enables people to do far more than see the alternative. Dialogue enables us to experience the alternative or certain aspects of it for a period of time and in a specific context. The real defeat of the oppressor within, the elimination from our thoughts and desires of all the "muck of bourgeois society," is what the process of socialism, or what Freire calls "cultural revolution," aims to achieve.

I have tried to select the ideas of Paulo Freire that offer the most important contributions to those working for social transformation. For those who, in the past, have either embraced him or dismissed him, as well as for others who have yet to encounter Freire's ideas, I can only hope this discussion has provided a useful challenge.

In the next section, I discuss Antonio Gramsci and his ideas and make comparative comments between Gramsci's ideas and those of Freire that I have just presented.

ANTONIO GRAMSCI

Gramsci was one of the founders of the Italian Communist Party and is acclaimed as a marxist scholar. He was imprisoned in 1926 by the first Fascist government in Europe. While in prison, a period that constituted the rest of his life, he undertook the writing of over 3,000 pages of notebooks in which he historically analysed the political and intellectual currents of Italian life and in which he suggested strategies for his Party. As with Freire's writings, most of Gramsci's writings, his prison notebooks (1971: hereafter *SPN*), correspondence and pre-prison political writings (1978: hereafter *SPW*) and cultural works are available in English translation. However, these writings vary considerably in their degree of clarity, and this can lead to problems and controversies over interpretation. Therefore, I begin this discussion of Gramsci's ideas with a suggestion regarding interpretation which should also help readers to draw comparisons with Freire and to assess the comparisons I make.

I would suggest that there are two essential ingredients that are needed to inform one's "reading" of Gramsci. First, Gramsci's analysis and ideas are firmly grounded in an understanding of Marx's dialectical theory of consciousness (see chapter 3). As I have already indicated, this is also the theoretical bedrock of Freire's ideas. The second ingredient pertains to one's approach to reading and studying Gramsci. This is an approach that Gramsci himself advocated. In discussing how we should interpret Marx's writings, Gramsci says something that is applicable equally to his own work:

> when one is dealing with a personality [Marx] in whom theoretical and practical activity are indissolubly intertwined and with an intellect in a process of continual creation and perpetual movement, with a strong and mercilessly vigorous sense of self-criticism. . . . Search for the *Leitmotiv* [guiding or leading motif] for the rhythm of the thought as it develops. [Gramsci, *SPN*, p. 383]

It is Gramsci's rhythm or guiding thread that I have attempted to identify and upon which I have based my interpretation of his ideas.

Gramsci, like many other communists of his time, was attempting, in his prison notebooks, to analyse why proletarian revolutions had not occurred in the West in the aftermath of the 1917 Bolshevik Revolution in Russia. His analysis appears to draw heavily on Marx's analysis of the bourgeois democratic state (Marx, 1843). From this analysis Gramsci concluded that there had to be two phases of revolution in the West. He explains (Gramsci, *SPN*, pp. 206–276) that in Western democracies power is experienced and consent engineered not just through the political state, as it was in prerevolutionary Russia, but also within the various organizations of civil society—for example, the family, church, trade unions and education (which falls within both the state and civil society). He uses the term 'hegemony," or moral, ethical leadership, to describe the means by which consent is organized. However, hegemony as a form of leadership can work primarily by either domination or direction (i.e., leading). In his analysis of how hegemony works in bourgeois civil society, he describes how it works primarily by domination or the imposition of ideological systems of belief as well as through the absorption of radical elements into the existing framework (pp. 57–59). On the other hand, when he uses the term hegemony with reference to "the war of position" or the socialist project to establish hegemony prior to the "war of movement," or revolution, he suggests a type of leadership that involves direction, vision and collaboration with the people rather than domination (pp. 133, 238–239, 241–243, 263, 267–268, 418). Of course, once political power is achieved, there would be the necessary domination of the enemies of the new order. Therefore, Gramsci conceptualizes hegemony as a combination of moral ethical direction and domination or a unity of consent and force. However, with socialist hegemony consent is not manipulated or managed but arrived at through critical choice.

One of the greatest sources of confusion in Gramsci's notebooks comes from his use of terms or concepts in two different senses. This is particularly true with his use of the terms "hegemony" and "ideology"; it is for this reason that it is so essential to follow his leitmotivs. I begin by first analyzing a brief section of the notebooks wherein readers would expect to find the meaning he attributed to the term "ideology." Then I return to a discussion of this problem in relation to his use of "hegemony"; "counter-hegemony," a term so often attributed to him, was never used, to my knowledge, by Gramsci. However, I hope the reason for that term will become clear in this discussion.

Before I undertook my own in-depth study of Gramsci and when I was attempting to arrive at a critical theorization of ideology, I had read many current marxist theorists' explanations of ideology (e.g., Hall, 1982; Simon, 1982). These authors encouraged me to think that ideological struggle involved the transformation of ideology—the challenge to an inferior ideology by a better, more comprehensive, socialist ideology. However, when I began to read Gramsci for myself, I could not agree. To start with, I could not agree in particular with one thing that Simon claims:

> In reading the Prison Notebooks it is helpful to bear in mind that Gramsci uses a variety of terms which for him are broadly equivalent to ideology, such as culture, philosophy, or world outlook or conception of the world as well as the phrase "moral and intellectual reform" when he is dealing with the transformation of ideology required for the advance to socialism. [Simon, 1982, p. 59]

Contrary to what Simon says, I thought that Gramsci was struggling to draw distinctions between ideas, particularly those that had to do with political strategies, and was not just using them interchangeably. My reading of Gramsci also indicated that he was using his prison notebooks to clarify his thinking. He was criticizing not just other people's ideas, but also his own previous thought and political practice (Gramsci, 1978, *SPW*). Most importantly, however, I did not think that he was trying to transform ideology in order to come up with an ideology appropriate for socialism but was trying to transform the meaning of ideology, the meaning of the word itself, when he used it in connection with Marxism or revolutionary strategy. Gramsci says:

> It however must be borne in mind that no new historical situation, however radical the change that has brought it about, completely transforms language, at least in its external formal aspect. But the content of the language must be changed. [Gramsci, 1971, *SPN*, p. 453]

In a few places, Gramsci signals that he is changing the meaning or content of the term "ideology" by referring alternatively to "ideology in the bad sense" or "ideology in the highest sense" (e.g. pp. 328, 407). However, he is not very consistent in doing so, and this makes any definitive interpretation of what he is saying, in one place or another, impossible. Therefore, Gramsci used "ideology" to refer to both something that is negative and something that is positive; however, his distinction arises from changing the actual meaning of "ideology" when he uses it to mean something positive (e.g. p. 356) rather than from contrasting competing explanations or systems of belief. Whether or not his approach in this respect leads to an appropriate strategy for social transformation is an important question. Therefore, I want to consider whether Gramsci's attempt to change the meaning of ideology was successful.

On pp. 375–377 of *SPN*, in a section entitled "The Concept of 'Ideology,'" he comes closest to a definition of this term. The only problem is that he offers two definitions, and it is open to interpretation as to which he considers " the bad sense." He starts off by saying that in eighteenth-century French materialism, ideology meant the science of ideas and that since science meant analysis, ideology actually meant "the investigation of the origin of ideas" (definition 1). Rather than rejecting that definition, he goes on to criticize the assumption in French materialism that ideas derived from sensations. He seems to be implying that the origin of ideas was being sought in the wrong place. He then offers a second definition by indirectly posing a question:

> How the concept of Ideology passed from meaning "science of ideas" and "analysis of the origin of ideas" to meaning specific "systems of ideas" [definition 2] needs to be examined historically. [p. 376]

So far, therefore, he has suggested two definitions, but in his next paragraph it is not clear to which of these he is referring; in fact, he seems to use both. First he says, "Freud is the last of the Ideologues," and just after this he says, "the author of the *Popular Manual* [Bukharin] has remained trapped in Ideology" (p. 376). The reference to Freud must pertain to his psychoanalysis of the "origin of ideas." However, if we consider that later in the notebooks Gramsci criticizes Bukharin for dispensing a mechanical, dogmatic, undialectical presentation of Marxism, then reference to his entrapment appears to refer to a "system of ideas" (pp. 417–472). This lack of clarity is extremely unfortunate, because in the next sentence Gramsci says:

> whereas the philosophy of praxis [the term Gramsci uses to refer to Marx's philosophy] represents a distinct advance and historically is precisely in opposition to Ideology. Indeed the meaning which the term "ideology" has assumed in Marxist philosophy implicity contains a negative value judgement and excludes the possibility that for its founders the origin of ideas should be sought for in sensations. [p. 376]

He seems to be saying that Marx and Engel's theory of ideology was a theory of the origin of ideas but not one that attributed that origin to sense impressions or any other physiological or psychological source. However, just when you think you might be reaching a clear idea about how Gramsci is changing the content of the term from "system of ideas" to the "analysis of the origin of ideas," he seems to begin discussing distinctions between different "systems of ideas."

> It seems to me that there is a potential element of error in assessing the value of ideologies, due to the fact (by no means casual) that the name ideology is given both to the necessary super-structure of a particular structure and to the arbitrary elucubrations of particular individuals. [p. 376]

Immediately before this, he has said: "'Ideology' itself must be analysed historically, in terms of the philosophy of praxis, as a superstructure." These passages could be read in two ways. One reading encourages the interpretation that ideology, including the "philosophy of praxis," is a system of ideas but, more precisely, a system of ideas that is organically necessary to a particular structure. Individual's ideologies are of no serious concern unless they are mistaken for organically necessary ones. So liberal-democratic (bourgeois) ideology would be necessary to British capitalism, and Marxist ideology would be organically necessary to socialism. This seems to be the way that Hall (1982) and many other Marxist writers interpret what Gramsci is saying. However, my reading is quite different.

Although it may appear that Gramsci is reverting to definition 2, "a system of ideas," I think he is actually developing his discussion of the real origin of ideas. The origin is either material reality, the structure, or "arbitrary elucubrations of individuals." So these are not refinements of definition 2. The task for "the philosophy of praxis" is to analyze the origin of ideas in the structure—to grasp the internal relations from which these ideas emerge. Marxist ideology, rather than being a system of ideas, would involve an analysis of reality, a "way of conceiving it," a way of understanding the structure that would enable people to change it. Therefore, it calls for a radical education project, as I have defined it. However, my interpretation is only feasible if you accept that Gramsci was changing the content of the term "ideology" when he used it in connection with Marxism, but was retaining its "bad sense"—a system of ideas—when referring to bourgeois ideology.

Unfortunately no one can offer a definitive interpretation of these three pages (pp. 375–377) from Gramsci's notebooks, simply because he is not clear. However, the two interpretations have important implications for strategy, particularly for interpreting what Gramsci was advocating for a revolutionary strategy. The most important implication pertains to the type of relationships that he advocates revolutionary leaders should establish with the people. Before discussing these, one further comment on this point about interpretations is necessary. From what Gramsci has said, we can see that he thought that ideologies were the organically necessary superstructure of a particular structure. We also know that he thought that "the philosophy of praxis" was an advance on existing ideology. However, the structure he is referring to is a capitalist one. So if Marxism is "an advance," this surely cannot refer to "a system of ideas" or a superstructure, because it arose prior to the existence of any socialist structure. It must refer to a way of understanding the origin of the existing "system of ideas," viz. bourgeois ideology. Fortunately, Gramsci had a great deal more to say about ideology than what he says on these three pages. In fact, you need to consider the rest of what he says in order to interpret this section. My later discussion of Gramsci's revolutionary strategy, in particular, should add further weight to the interpretation I have just given of his concept of ideology. Furthermore, Marx's theory of consciousness contains a critical, negative concept of ideology and existing ideologies or systems of belief, and, if you recall, I contend that Gramsci's thinking is fundamentally grounded in that theory.

As I have discussed, sometimes Gramsci signaled the shift in meaning by referring to ideology in the "highest sense" or, alternatively, in the "bad sense," but these signals are rare. The same problem pertains to his use of the term "hegemony." With this qualification and his distinction between leadership primarily by domination or alternatively direction in mind, I find striking parallels between what Paulo Freire and Gramsci propose as a strategy for revolution or transformative cultural action.

Gramsci's writings are also underpinned by an assumption of what it currently means to be human and what it could mean. Like Freire, he derives these assumptions from Marx. In a section entitled "What is Man?" Gramsci explains:

> Reflecting on it, we can see that in putting the question "what is man?" what we mean is: what can [humanity] become? That is can [people] dominate [their] own destiny, can [they] "make [themselves]", can [they] create [their] own life? We maintain therefore that [people are] a process, and more exactly, the process of [their] actions. . . . one must conceive of [human beings] as a series of active relationships [with other people and nature]. . . . If one's own individuality is the *ensemble* of these relations, to create one's personality means to acquire consciousness of them and to modify one's personality means to modify the *ensemble* of these relations. [*SPN*, pp. 351–352]

From this it is clear that Gramsci shares with Marx and Freire the notion that what we are as human beings—our human nature—does not exist prior to our relationships with other people and our natural and social circumstances. Furthermore, we can become conscious of the historically specific nature of our current relations and can actively, in association with other people, create new relations within which we could realize our human potential to plan and direct our historical future. Taking into consideration the limitations that the current ensemble of relations places on our consciousness (limited praxis), Gramsci reminds us that so far in history what unites human beings is *not* their capacity for thought: "It is not 'thought' but what people really think that unites or differentiates [humankind]" (p. 355). He also stresses that the current ensemble of human relations is based on dialectical contradictions:

> Indeed social relations are expressed by various groups of [people] which each presuppose the others and whose unity is dialectical. . . . Man is aristocratic in so far as man is serf, etc. [p. 355]

I have suggested that Freire understood Marxism to be a method of analysis that he refers to alternatively as science, critical perception or dialectical analysis. Gramsci also equates Marxism with a method of analysis. However he uses the term "philosophy of praxis" to refer to both Marx's method and his "conception of the world," viz. "that of a human race united the world over" (p. 324). However, he sets the "philosophy of praxis" apart from all other philosophies primarily on methodological and epistemological grounds:

> In a sense, moreover, the philosophy of praxis is a reform and a development of Hegelianism; it is a philosophy that has been liberated (or is attempting to liberate itself) from any unilateral and fanatical ideological elements; it is consciousness full of contradictions [dialectical ones], in which the philosopher himself . . . not only grasps the contradictions but posits himself as an element of the contradiction. . . . [pp. 404–405]

And later in the notebooks he says of the "philosophy of praxis":

> The Hegelian "idea" [the dialectic] has been resolved both in structure and in the superstructures and the whole way of conceiving philosophy has been "historised," that is to say a new way of philosophising which is more concrete and historical than what went before it. . . . [p. 448]

The last quote comes from a section of the notebooks where Gramsci, in criticizing Bukharin's *Popular Manual*, offers his clearest articulation of his own understanding of Marx's ideas. When read in its totality, this section makes it clear that Gramsci had fully understood that Marx's materialism was epistemologically revolutionary and was entirely distinct from past forms of materialism. Apart from trying to evade the prison censor, I suspect that Gramsci's use of the expression "philosophy of praxis," rather than dialectical or historical materialism, was also part of his polemic with deterministic and mechanical interpretations of Marx, such as those contained in the *Popular Manual* (*SPN*, pp. 419–472).

Another element that links the ideas of Freire and Gramsci is their understanding that for Marx there are different types or levels of consciousness. Gramsci distinguishes especially between common sense, ideology and the philosophy of praxis. He stresses that all people are philosophers in that they hold some conception of the world. However, common sense is fragmented due to the limitations and contradictions of our lived relations. Ideologies (in the bad sense) may draw upon these fragments offering partial explanations, but they do so with a coherence capable of organizing people and cementing the hegemony of a particular ruling group (pp. 197–198, 324–325, 404–405). As we have just seen, Gramsci considered the "philosophy of praxis" to be the pinnacle of philosophical achievement. He also refers to it as "a superior conception of the world, scientifically and coherently elaborated—i.e. knowledge" (p. 418). So it provides a coherence, as does ideology, but instead it is a scientific—that is, nonideological or dialectical—coherence. In fact, earlier in the notebooks he insists that "the philosophy of praxis represents a distinct advance and historically is precisely in opposition to Ideology" (p. 376).

In terms of a socialist political strategy, Gramsci seems to be implying that political leaders should utilize ideology (i.e. its highest sense, the analysis of the origin of ideas) to problematize people's already existing thought (i.e. common sense) so that all people can become philosophers of praxis. Therefore, Gramsci's political strategy is based on a radical/critical education process. Before documenting the passages that imply this strategy, it is important to note that the strategical implication deriving from these three levels of consciousness can be (and has been) interpreted differently. For readers who do not accept that Gramsci uses the term ideology in two different senses, who interpret him to use it only to mean a coherent system of beliefs, then "the philosophers of praxis" are only those people whom Gramsci refers to as the "organic intellectuals" of the working class or an even more select vanguard of political leaders. It is they who engage in the dialectical analysis of reality and who translate it into a coherent system of beliefs (ideology) capable of organizing the consent and the action of the people. Given some passages in the notebooks, this interpretation is entirely possible. However, I would argue that it leads to an inappropriate strategy, and that it also conflicts with Gramsci's guiding thread.

In discussing what a "theory of the philosophy of praxis" would entail, Gramsci says that it would have to deal with several questions, including "What are the relationships between ideologies, concepts of the world and philosophies?" (p. 425). His editors/translators comment that it is this question and the others that Gramsci is attempting to answer in the philosophical sections of the notebooks. In those sections, Gramsci stresses that "It is essential to destroy the widespread prejudice that philosophy [is the preserve of the specialist]" (p. 323). After arguing that everyone is a philosopher because he or she holds a conception of the world, he asks:

> is it better to "think", without critical awareness, in a disjointed and episodic way [common sense]? In other words is it better to take part in a conception of the world mechanically imposed by the external environment, i.e. by one of the many social groups in which everyone is automatically involved. . . . Or, on the other hand, is it better to work out consciously and critically one's own conception of the world and thus, in connection with the labour of one's own brain, choose one's sphere of activity, take an active part in the creation of the history of the world, be one's own guide, refusing to accept passively and supinely from outside the moulding of one's personality? [pp. 323–324]

If you remember that, for Gramsci, the philosophy of praxis is both a method of analysis and a conception of the world, then this passage must surely apply equally to Marx's conception of the world. Later he establishes the relationship between philosophy and common sense (it is clear that he is talking about the philosophy of praxis): "Philosophy is criticism and the superseding of . . . 'common sense'. In this sense it coincides with 'good' as opposed to 'common' sense" (p. 326). Frequently he stresses that this type of philosophy must be the preserve of everyone. For example:

> For a mass of people to be led to think coherently and in the same coherent fashion about the real present world is a "philosophical" event far more

important and "original" than the discovery by some philosophical "genius" of a truth which remains the property of small groups of intellectuals. [p. 325]

Although "the philosophers of praxis" at first may be a small group, their task is to help or lead others so that they might develop this way of thinking about or understanding their world.

To criticise one's own conception of the world means therefore to make it a coherent unity and to raise it to the level reached by the most advanced thought in the world [Marx's]. [p. 324]

He goes on to argue that if intellectuals form a dialectical unity (non-antagonistic) with the people, they will be organic intellectuals. After criticizing the "Popular Universities" [Italian institutions a bit like the British Workers' Educational Association] for failing to be organic, he says:

That is, if the intellectuals had been organically the intellectuals of the masses, and if they had worked out and made coherent the principles and problems raised by the masses in their practical activity, thus constituting a cultural and social bloc [then they would have been effective]. The question posed here [is] . . . is a philosophical movement properly so called when it is devoted to creating a specialised culture amongst restricted social groups, or rather when, and only when, in the process of elaborating a form of thought superior to "common sense" and *coherent on a scientific plane* [my emphasis], it never forgets to remain in contact with the "simple" and indeed finds in this content the source of the problems, it sets out to study and resolve? . . . A philosophy of praxis cannot but present itself at the outset in a polemical and critical guise, as superseding the existing mode of thinking and existing concrete thought.... First of all, therefore, it must be a criticism of "common sense", basing itself initially however on common sense in order to demonstrate that "everyone" is a philosopher and that it is not a question of introducing from scratch a scientific form of thought into everyone's individual life, but of renovating and making "critical" an already existing activity. [pp. 330–331]

This passage may well be one of self-criticism. In his writings between 1921–26, Gramsci stressed the need for the party to educate the working class and the peasants in terms of Marxist theory. At that time he actually advocated the use of Bukharin's manual (Gramsci, *SPW*, pp.

283–292), which he extensively criticizes in the prison notebooks (*SPN*, pp. 419–472) for its dogmatic, undialectical positivism. In his years of active political life, Gramsci was keenly aware that the revolution would only succeed in containing the forces of counter-revolution if it had the solid support of the majority of the working class behind it and if that majority had established its hegemony (leadership) with the poor peasants (Gramsci, *SPW*, pp. 441–462). However, it was through his own self-critical reflections in his prison writings that he struggled to develop a more complex strategy for working with people in a way that could forge a collective will for revolution. I would suggest that Gramsci's self-criticism is most strongly reflected in phrases such as "To criticise one's own conception of the world" (Gramsci, *SPN*, p. 324), as well as in the last phrase of the preceding quotation: "renovating and making 'critical' an already existing activity." It seems quite clear to me that if Gramsci is being consistent/coherent, the intellectuals or original philosophers of praxis are not the "renovators" or the "makers" but, rather, everyone is. The leader's or radical educator's role is to persuade and encourage people to undertake these renovations and to help them question their already existing activity (common-sense thinking) until it becomes "critical" activity (dialectical thinking). Again, in the preceding passage I find parallels with Freire that are striking.

The educator or political activist begins with people's concrete perceptions of the world (their limited praxis) and helps them to come to a critical, scientific or, in other words, dialectical conceptualization. Freire offers greater detail than Gramsci on how to learn and think with other people, but in the following passage Gramsci advocates the same sort of transformed relations between teachers and students as does Freire. In the first part, Gramsci also gives an indication of just how expansive and deeply rooted the socialist hegemonic project must be.

> An historic act can only be performed by "collective man", and this presupposes the attainment of a "cultural-social" unity through which a multiplicity of dispersed wills, with heterogeneous aims, are welded together with a single aim, on the basis of an equal and common conception of the world, both general and particular, . . . where the intellectual base is so well rooted, assimilated and experienced that it becomes passion. . . .
>
> This problem can and must be related to the modern [Marx's] way of considering educational doctrine and practice, according to which the relation between teacher and pupil is active and reciprocal so that every teacher is always a pupil and every pupil a teacher. But the educational relationship

should not be restricted to the field of strictly "scholastic" relationships. . . . This form of relationship exists throughout society as a whole and for every individual relative to other individuals. . . . Every relation of "hegemony" is necessarily an educational relationship. . . . [pp. 349–350]

Note that, in this instance, Gramsci places the term "hegemony" in quotation marks. It could be that he did so to highlight his distinction between hegemony primarily through direction and reciprocal relations, as opposed to hegemony by domination. It seems fairly clear that he is referring throughout this passage to socialist rather than bourgeois hegemony. Gramsci certainly appears to be quite aware that a social–historical movement aimed at abolishing classes demands an entirely different type of educational relationship. Here he has stressed the teacher–pupil and the leadership relations. However, if we consider what he has said in the earlier passages about the critique of common sense, which he later extends to include "all previous philosophy" (p. 350), it would appear that he, like Freire, also advocates a changed relationship to knowledge. In fact, in several places in his notebooks (e.g. p. 456) Gramsci indicates that Marx offered an entirely new theory of consciousness and therefore knowledge—that is, epistemology—and as I have suggested in my discussion of Freire this new theory of necessity would demand a new relation to knowledge.

It should not be surprising that Gramsci and Freire, two Marxist thinkers, advocate a changed relation to knowledge. Marx's theory of consciousness/praxis marked both an epistemological and an ontological revolution—revolutions in the way we think about "knowledge" and "being" and the relation between them.

So far I have suggested that there is a compatibility between Freire's and Gramsci's ideas. The idea that a period of preparation or prefiguration is necessary to revolutionary struggle is central to both their thinking. Gramsci is often credited with this invention or contribution to Marx's thought. However, in a letter to German socialists, Marx too had stressed the need for preparation, or what Freire refers to as cultural action. He warned:

The point of view of the minority is dogmatic instead of critical, idealistic instead of materialistic. They regard not the real conditions but a *mere effort of will* as the driving force of revolution. Whereas we say to the workers: "You will have to go through 15, 20, 50 years of civil wars and national struggles not only to bring about change in society but also to change yourselves, and prepare yourselves for the experience of political power." [Marx, 1853, pp. 402–403]

Freire and Gramsci both stress the importance of *will*, but not the solipsistic type that Marx is criticizing. For Gramsci,

> in the last analysis [will] equals practical or political activity . . . it must be rational, not an arbitrary, will, which is realised in so far as it corresponds to objective historical necessities. . . . [Gramsci, *SPN*, p. 345]

He later elaborates on this:

> If the relations between . . . leaders and led . . . is provided by an organic cohesion in which feeling-passion becomes understanding and thence knowledge . . . Only then . . . can the shared life be realised which alone is a social force—with the creation of the "historical bloc." [p. 418]

For Freire, the will for revolution develops within prerevolutionary cultural projects; it stems primarily from the critical perception of reality that these projects aim to develop. Even if people's passion has been numbed, the critical perception can arouse it (Freire, 1972, especially p. 58).

A further contribution that Gramsci made to Marxism was the idea of "forming alliances." I think that this idea is often interpreted naively. For Gramsci, the main alliances to be forged were between poor peasants, agricultural wage laborers and industrial workers. In other words, the alliances were to be between those who were creating surplus value and those who were potential candidates for exploitation within the labor–capital relation. Also included were intellectuals of bourgeois origin who relocated themselves with the interest of socialist revolution. However, he was adamant, as were most members of the Italian Communist Party during the 1920s, against forming alliances with other antifascist forces who had reformist tendencies such as those exhibited by the Italian Socialist Party. Despite concerted Comintern pressure, they stood firmly opposed to either fusing with or forming a "United Front" with the Socialist Party. Their tactic was a united front from below, whereby in creating organizations in which all workers could participate, regardless of party or union affiliation, they hoped through argument and leadership or example to encourage the majority of the working class to affiliate with the Communist Party (Gramsci, *SPW*, pp. 287 ff., 400–411).

Gramsci and Freire contribute something new to Marx's thought by discussing in detail how socialist educators, or political activists, or any other cultural workers for social transformation should work *with* people prior to the moment of revolution. Clearly there are parts in both of their writings which have led some interpreters to view Gramsci as the rigorous, no-nonsense, authentic revolutionary and Freire as no more than a liberal, humanist pedagogue. I can only suggest that such interpretations ignore the leitmotiv of Freire's writings and do him a great injustice. The consequence of ignoring either Freire's or Gramsci's leitmotiv is worse still, because the broad-based movement that we need to develop for social transformation will be denied a theoretical mode of action for working together *with* people for a just and humanized future. It also bars us from engaging in an analysis, based on our own context, of whether the initiator of that broad-based movement should be the party (a political party) as Gramsci advocated or some other form of organization that might initially ally marxists who are members of different political parties and social movements. The need for this analysis is urgent.

There is one issue, pertaining to strategy, on which there appears to be a considerable difference between Freire and Gramsci. It raises important questions, because it has to do with just how extensive prefiguration must be for revolution to be successful. Due to the nonexistence of a well-organized revolutionary party in his context (i.e., Brazil in the 1960s), Freire distinguished between the limited nature of educational projects during the prefigurative stage of cultural action and the expansive and systematic project of cultural revolution. Unfortunately, Gramsci's concept of the extensiveness of prefigurative work is not clear and may have been so intimately linked to his own conditions that it cannot be generalized to others.

In his discussion of the war of position, Gramsci equates it with a formula for "civil hegemony" (Gramsci, *SPN*, p. 243). Earlier in the notebooks where he is analyzing the nature of bourgeois hegemony, he emphasizes that:

> A social group can, and indeed must, already exercise "leadership" before winning governmental power. . . . there can and must be a "political

hegemony" even before the attainment of governmental power. . . . [p. 57, 57 fn.]

These passages seem to imply that socialism will have to have become the "good sense" of the vast majority of people prior to the revolutionary moment of taking power. The party, or broad-based movement that allies all marxists, would have to have attained a position of leadership in all sections of civil society. From a current perspective, this seems an extremely extensive prefigurative project, but just how extensive actually hinges upon Gramsci's definition of civil society. Once again we are faced with an unclear definition. Hoare and Smith, his editors/translators, point out (in *SPN*, pp. 207–209) that sometimes he includes the mode of economic behavior in civil society, following Marx's usage of the term, but at other times he locates civil society as standing between the economic structure and the state. However, Gramsci says at least in one place that such distinctions between structures are not organic but merely methodological (p. 160). Again, we must consider his leitmotiv, which on balance appears to include the mode of economic behavior as part of civil society.

At present, Gramsci's proposed strategy simply seems too ambitious to realize in most contexts. Hoare and Smith also point out (in *SPN*) that this is one of the

> supreme paradoxes of Gramsci's thought, a dilemma to which he found no answer. For there is precisely a dissimilarity between the situation of the bourgeoisie under feudalism or pre-bourgeois forms of State and that of the proletariat under bourgeois rule. In the former case, capitalist relations of production can develop within the feudal State, until at a certain point in time the "carapace" cracks. In the latter case, however, this is not so. It is quite impossible for socialist relations of production to develop "within" capitalism. . . . Clearly these problems are closely related too to Gramsci's statement that "A social group can, and indeed must, already 'lead' [i.e. be hegemonic] before winning governmental power (this indeed is one of the principal conditions for the winning of such power)." [p. 47]

I would not deny that with appropriate organization a great deal could be done and must be done to infuse a majority of people with socialist "good sense" or a critical understanding of capitalism and a will for socialism. But I also think that every advance made in that direction will of necessity create movements in capital's bourgeois hegemony and ideology. These movements will alter between concession or conciliation and force; therefore, our own movements will have to be based on a critical reading of the situation. But, in every instance, it seems to me that prior to revolution our project is an oppositional one—that is, a critique of existing conditions, a counter-hegemonic project, based on small-scale projects that offer the experience of transformed relations—rather than a predominantly hegemonic one. In fairness, there are parts of Gramsci's notebooks that also seem to suggest this and to question the degree to which "civil hegemony" can be accomplished prior to revolution. I think that the confusion that arises from Gramsci's notebooks regarding this important question of strategy arises from two factors. The first was Gramsci's experience of the Factory Councils in Turin in 1919–1920, together with the absence (at least in the selections of the notebooks available in English) of any sustained critical analysis of that experience. The second factor is the way in which Gramsci appears to formulate his strategy from a historical analysis of bourgeois hegemony. I will consider each of these factors in turn.

In April 1919, Gramsci and others founded a weekly review of socialist culture, the *Ordine Nuovo*. They had little idea at that time that this paper would become an organizational and educational force for the urban proletariat and one of the key elements for encouraging the idea of revolution. That "idea" culminated in September 1920 in Factory Councils springing up throughout many areas of Italian industry. These councils were autonomous organizations of the workers—independent from the traditional organizations of trade unions and political parties. When the Romeo plant threatened a lockout, the workers occupied the factory, and the tactic spread quickly, soon assuming "a scale and character which far exceeded anybody's expectations" (p. xliii). (This summary is taken from Hoare and Smith's "General Introduction" in *SPN*.) However when it came to the revolutionary conjuncture no group was in a position to assume leadership. The Italian Socialist Party (PSI; the Communist Party had not yet been founded) and the trade unions wanted a compromise solution, and the Turin representatives of the Factory Councils, who were the best organized and who had to some degree armed their factories, knew that their military preparation fell far short of what was necessary for revolution. Compromise was offered by the Italian government, and not long afterward the forces of reaction set in as fascist squads began their raids against various socialist organizations and strongholds.

The Factory Councils were organizations that workers had set up spontaneously. It would appear that Gramsci derived his idea of how the party should be dialectically linked to the people from his relations with the Factory Councils of Turin. In speaking of his relation with the Turin movement, which was accused of being "spontaneist" and "voluntarist," he says:

> the leadership given to the movement was both creative and correct. This leadership was not "abstract"; it neither consisted in mechanically repeating scientific or theoretical formulae, nor did it confuse politics, real action, with theoretical disquisition. It applied itself to real [people], formed in specific historical relations, with feelings, outlooks, fragmentary conceptions of the world, etc., which were the "spontaneous" combinations of a given situation of material production with the "fortuitous" agglomeration within it of disparate social elements. This element of "spontaneity" was not neglected and even less despised. It was *educated*, directed, purged of extraneous contaminations; the aim was to bring it into line with modern theory [Marxism]—but in a living and historically effective manner. . . . It gave the masses a "theoretical" consciousness of being the creators of *historical* and institutional *values*, of being founders of a State. This unity between "spontaneity" and "conscious leadership" or "discipline" is precisely the real political action of the subaltern classes, in so far as this is mass politics and not merely an adventure by groups claiming to represent the masses. [*SPN*, p. 198]

Therefore, Gramsci had had the real experience of not a party but a newspaper (established by those who would later form the Communist Party) working in dialectical unity with the people. He had also witnessed the degree to which the Factory Councils had "created institutional values" or presumably ethical and political leadership—that is, hegemony—within factory life. This must have been one of the factors that led him to assume that hegemony even within the economic sphere of production could be and would have to be established prior to the revolutionary moment. From his analysis of the "modern prince"—that is, the Communist Party—it would appear that Gramsci thought that the Factory Councils only failed because of the absence of an appropriate revolutionary party (pp. 125–205).[8] Another reason why Gramsci thought that the revolutionary party was so crucial was that it would be needed to ally the peasants and agricultural workers, who were located primarily in southern Italy, to the leadership of the industrial proletariat of the north. Only if history were to repeat itself in an exact manner could we know if his analysis was correct.

However, to return to my earlier point regarding opposition or counter-hegemony rather than hegemony, it seems to me that any such direct move for hegemonic control of production, prior to revolution, will of necessity lead to direct confrontation with the forces of capital. I would suggest, in agreement with Hoare and Smith (in *SPN*, p. 47), that Gramsci's strategy for revolution may have relied too heavily on his historical analysis of how the bourgeoisie had established their hegemony. From that analysis he concluded that the bourgeoisie was able to elicit the unquestioning consent of the mass of the population because of the dominant role it played in economic affairs (p. 12). This ignores the crucial difference between the emergence of the capitalist social formation and that of a socialist transition to the communist social form. Capitalism was a progressive variation on a theme. It was a progressive form of exploitation or a progressive mode of one group extracting the surpluses produced by another. Through trade and commerce, the bourgeoisie built up its prestige and confidence and a degree of hegemony within social life prior to instituting the specific capitalist mode and relations of production and prior to wresting the bulk of political power from the landed aristocracy. Bourgeois ideas, bourgeois ideology, had wide appeal even to other classes because they did represent improvements on feudal conditions, especially feudalism's potential for generating wealth (Marx and Engels, 1846, pp. 40–41). This bourgeois progress entailed a specific type of freedom—freedom from a system of privileges and duties and freedom to make wealth or go bankrupt, and so forth. It was also about abstract notions of equality that had real appeal to those who were not equal and knew they were not.

On the other hand, socialist revolution has a much more complex task to perform. It must involve a total revolution of the relations of production and the objectives of production and therefore a revolution in people too. Socialists cannot, as the bourgeoisie did, become dominant or hegemonic within civil society, social *and economic life*, prior to revolution. However, this is not to imply that socialists working through movements such as the Factory Councils could not through ethical and moral leadership and dialogical education establish a broad-based will for socialism. I am suggesting that the establishing of socialist hegemony must be handled very carefully; at every moment the movements of capital must be analyzed and predicted. The bourgeoisie were not the dialectical opposite of the feudal lords—the serfs were. Therefore, their movements did not of necessity bring an immediate reaction from the powerful of the social formation they were to replace. The reverse is the truth of our struggle. By all means, with appropriate organization, cultural activists working for authentic social transformation can engage in leading, educating, working with people in all areas of civil society prior to revolution. However, at the point at which they are ready to become hegemonic, to lead, particularly within production, they must also be ready for revolution.

I have raised these points about the extent to which Gramsci was suggesting that the project for "civil hegemony" should be taken because I think that they have important implications for transformative strategy as we begin the next millenium. In Britain in the 1980s, a great deal of intellectual work was devoted to using Gramsci's concept of hegemony to analyze both the appropriate strategy for socialism as well as neoconservatism's success in establishing a new hegemonic consensus. Stuart Hall, for example, wrote many excellent articles for *Marxism Today*. In my opinion, these hegemonic projects need to be analyzed dialectically because they relate back to two of the most fundamental dialectical contradictions of capitalism: viz. that between productive labor and capital and that between production and exchange. I would suggest that neoconservatism's hegemonic project was aimed at safeguarding the interests of the most advanced and, in capitalist terms, progressive capitalist organizations. If this suggestion is correct, it is important to consider, in a more dialectically conscious way, what the strategy of the restless negatives should be vis-à-vis that of their opposite. And that consideration must also include an analysis of just who the restless negatives are (see my earlier discussion in chapter 4 of Marx's dialectical conceptualization of class).

I have tried to persuade you that Gramsci's and Freire's ideas are important to struggles for a socialist future, the one I presented as "The Vision" in chapter 2. But, in the last analysis, I would urge that these ideas be used not to dictate strategies but to inform and guide the development of a critical/revolutionary praxis based on a dialectical understanding of our present conditions. Surely Gramsci and Freire, or any other critical (dialectical) thinker, would never advise otherwise.

NOTES

1. Some aspects of this section have appeared previously in my article "Paulo Freire's Contribution to Radical Adult Education," *Studies in the Education of Adults*, *26*, No. 2 (1994), pp. 144–161.

2. A great deal of progressive adult education has been influenced by the psychologists of "personal freedom" such as Carl Rogers. Rogers himself has claimed affinity with Freire, and in educational journals there have been numerous articles that attempt to conflate the ideas of Freire and Rogers. Two learning colleagues (students), James Calvey and Janet Galpin, have written excellent Diploma dissertations that demolish these claims.

3. Complementary reading: P. Freire, *The Politics of Education* (London: Macmillan, 1985), p. 162, where he says: "Marx underlined, in *The Holy Family*, the conscious action of the proletariat in the abolition of themselves as a class by the abolition of the objective conditions that constitute that class." (When I quote Freire and later Gramsci, I alter their use of gender language by using whenever I can, without distorting the meaning, plural nouns and pronouns.)

4. Writers' and Readers' Publishing Co-operative published their edition in 1976; due to the publication date, it is often thought that this text postdates *Pedagogy of the Oppressed*, but in fact it was written in 1967.

5. See also Freire, *Politics of Education*, pp. 160–162.

6. Bourgeois education is education that has developed within or been further developed within capitalist social relations.

7. To reiterate: Freire uses an anthropological definition of the term "culture." He is not just referring to "high" culture but also to every material object and every aspect of social consciousness that is produced by the social being of people living within a specific cultural variation of a social formation.

8. Here, Gramsci discusses "The Modern Prince"—that is, the Communist Party.

REFERENCES

Allman, P., and Wallis, J. (1990). "Praxis: Implications for 'Really' Radical Education." *Studies in Adult Education*, *22*, No. 1, 14–30.

Freire, P. (1972). *Pedagogy of the Oppressed.* Harmondsworth: Penguin.

Freire, P. (1974a). *Authority versus Authoritarianism.* Audiotape in the series "Thinking with Paulo Freire." Sydney, Australia: Australian Council of Churches.

Freire, P. (1974b). "Education: Domestication or Liberation." In I. Lister (Ed.), *De-Schooling.* Cambridge: Cambridge University Press.

Freire, P. (1976). *Education: The Practice of Freedom.* London: Writers' and Readers' Publishing Co-operative.

Freire, P. (1985). *The Politics of Education.* London: Macmillan.

Gramsci, A. (1971). *Selections from the Prison Notebooks of Antonio Gramsci,* edited and translated by Quinton Hoare and Geoffrey Nowell Smith. London: Lawrence and Wishart.

Gramsci, A. (1978). *Selections from Political Writings 1921–1926,* edited and translated by Quinton Hoare. London: Lawrence and Wishart.

Hall, S. (1982). "Managing Conflict, Producing Consent." Unit 21, in Block 5: *Conformity, Consensus and Conflict, D102, Social Sciences: A Foundation Course.* Milton Keynes: Open University Press.

Marx, K. (1843). "On the Jewish Question." In D. McLellan (Ed.), *Karl Marx: Selected Writings* (pp. 39–62). Oxford: Oxford University Press, 1977.

Marx, K. (1853). "Revelations Concerning the Communist Trial in Cologne." In *Karl Marx and Frederick Engels Collected Works, Vol. 11.* Moscow: Progress Publishers, 1979.

Marx, K. and Engels, F. (1845). *The Holy Family.* London: Lawrence and Wishart, 1956.

Marx, K., and Engels, F. (1846). *The German Ideology.* Moscow: Progress Publishers, 1976.

Simon, R. (1982). *Gramsci's Political Thought.* London: Lawrence and Wishart.

6

More on Visions: Re-Creating Our Concepts of Democracy, Truth and Equality

In chapter 2, I utilized Marx's ideas to present the basic elements of "the vision" of a humanized future. Of course, this is only one among many visions that we could create, but, as I said, it is the one that guides my thinking and analysis and therefore the entire book, including this chapter. Here, I want to examine three very important concepts and the experience that has led to them; however, I will also suggest some ways by which we could begin to rethink them and eventually re-create the meaning of them through a more humanized existence. I have chosen democracy, truth and equality not only because they are fundamental to our thinking about the future, but also because they are frequently used in a naturalized or unproblematical manner—as if we all know what we mean and desire. Many more concepts need to be reexamined and, if necessary, re-created; I simply want to get the ball rolling by sharing my ideas about these three. Eventually we will need a collective and collaborative project aimed at creating a vision that can unite our wills and energies.

DEMOCRACY

The historical roots of the concept or ideal of democracy are usually located in ancient Athens. The Athenians are admired for creating a form of "direct democracy" in which every citizen participated in the governance of the city state. However, the degree to which this governing worked in those ancient conditions depended on a very restricted concept of citizenship. Slaves and free women were not included, even though they contributed a great deal to the society. A restricted concept of the meaning of citizen has accompanied the development of democracy as it spread to other areas of the world. Struggles by those excluded from citizenship underpin the entire historical development of democracy. Many people argue that concessions to citizenship are won only when one excluded group or another gains inclusion because they have been effectively subdivided off from other excluded people or when the rights, responsibilities and powers they were struggling for have become "de-valued" or in effect unimportant as tools for actually challenging the social structure and initiating social transformation. There is abundant historical evidence to support this pessimism, whether we consider struggles against property qualifications or those for inclusion of women and black people. Although I appreciate the importance of these struggles, I must question whether the struggle for inclusion into the given forms of democracy was ever enough on its own. I would argue that such struggles should have been linked to and integrated with a struggle to transform the actual experience and consequent meaning of democracy.

By the time in history when various disenfranchized groups found the courage and conviction to struggle for inclusion, the systems or forms of democracy were largely representative democracies. As we all know, this means that we vote for the people to whom we devolve our powers to govern. Of course, they are supposed to be accountable, but we can only register our assessment of their representative performances in an effective way by the next vote or, in some cases (and again after a time interval), by what in Britain is called the deselection of a current politician in terms of future candidacy.

However, even in the late eighteenth century and the nineteenth century some novel and perhaps potentially progressive ideas developed within small pockets of the experience of representative democracy. The two that come to mind seem miles apart on various counts, but they do share some common features. The original idea behind the United States House of Representatives was that all citizens should devote two years of their lives to taking responsibility, if they were elected, for governance. The ideal was as short-lived as my second example, the

Paris Commune of the early 1870s. In this case, commune members were expected to take turns in both making and executing the laws. It was a type of work and contribution to the society like any other and remunerated at the same level. Representatives, at any one time, were also subject to immediate recall if the commune members felt that they were not governing effectively or justly. As I said, the idea in the first case and the commune itself were short-lived. Nevertheless, they were novel approaches to re-creating democracy in a more democratized form, a form in which we might begin to reabsorb some of our political powers into our daily existence and the expression of our humanity. However, there is little evidence of any such innovations in our own time. It appears that we have capitulated at the very moment in history when "democracy" is claimed to have become the universal ideal because of the supposed necessary relation between democracy and the "free market."

I question both the universality of the ideal and the contemporaneousness of the capitulation. The history of the development of modern democracy is a history of capitulation and compromise. Hall (1982) explains that many of the concepts that underpin the modern forms of democracy were originally associated with the emergence of market exchange. "Equality" pertained to the idea that, in exchange, equivalent values were passed from buyers to sellers, and vice versa. "Freedom" referred to the breaking of feudal bonds in the sale and employment of labor, the emergence of the "free" wage laborer and employers who were "free" to become rich or go bankrupt. It was also associated with people being "free" to express their choices by exiting from one market site in favor of another rather than expressing their choices by exercising their voices and engaging in struggles to transform the conditions they consider to be undesirable (Bowles and Gintis, 1986). Therefore, when these concepts emerged within the democratic ideal, they already had a history of the limited and restricted sense in which they had been experienced by people in market exchange.

As I indicated before, market exchange or "free" unregulated markets are currently linked to the argument that democracy has become the universal ideal. It is assumed that democracy will be the inevitable outcome of most people desiring and continuing to desire (another assumption) "free-market" economies. The coupling of markets and democracy ignores a great deal of historical specificity as well as the current evidence that reveals the existence of markets, market economies, in either the total absence of democratic governance (e.g. China) or such restricted forms of democracy that we consider them democracies in name only. Also, of course, we must remember that this consideration is based only on a comparison with our modern and very limited concept of democracy. I never would argue that the rights and responsibilities that many of us enjoy would not be of benefit to people who experience the total absence of democracy or democracy in extremely limited forms. However, to focus on those potential struggles alone often deflects our thinking from an authentic effort to re-create our concept of democracy and our related efforts to establish it in the various sites of our daily existence.

I admire the ideal of the U.S. House of Representatives and the Paris Commune because they were underpinned by a very important concept that is rarely associated with democracy—the concept of time. I am convinced that re-creating our use of time is absolutely essential to re-creating democracy. Each of us would need to devote some time during the day, or week, or a section of our life to engaging in active political and social participation in our communities and the wider society. For this work, we should be remunerated "according to our needs" like any other productive worker who contributes to society. It goes without saying that this only can happen when we decide to totally transform our societies so that we produce or work to meet human need rather than to create profit.

I hope that these ideas do not seem utopian; I previously promised that all my "utopian" visions have some grounding in our current or recent realities. For example, for many years I have worked in a department of adult and continuing education as a full-time, salaried, professional worker. I have always believed that my responsibilities included not just a full commitment to teaching and research, but also participation in political and social projects that contributed to the life of communities. I would never have expected or asked for remuneration for this work; it was part of my work and the expression of the principles I hold concerning the purpose of adult education. In the present climate, it is more difficult to do this. Everything I do and plan to do has to be precisely documented and is carefully monitored. Even research (of the type that was necessary for this book), which is part of the job remit, is no longer as highly valued as that which attracts outside funding. Needless to say, contributions within the community are valued only when they too can bring in, or promise to bring in, additional money. However, I have known, experienced, another way of working and will never give up the hope that the fulfilment it brings could be generalized within the life experience of all people. There would be one very significant difference: I was *allowed* to or ignored when I participated in these other activities, whereas my vision of a transformed society is one in which we are encouraged, enabled, supported and valued for engaging in social and political service.

This aspect of my thinking has direct relevance to current social circumstances wherein some influential politicians are trying to put employment at the top of the political agenda and when so many millions of people are desperate for them to do so. Others argue that full employment, defined in any sense, is no longer a possibility if their economies are to be based on the "cutting edge" of technological advance and global competition, both of which normally mean fewer jobs. However, their arguments assume capitalist social relations of production and production for profit, rather than production or work directed at meeting human needs and doing so outside market relations. In contrast, I argue that we could perceive and realize our goals differently. We could use technology within different social relations to allow each of us enough time away from producing useful products for human consumption to actively engage in producing a social order in which we experience and come, *en masse*, to enjoy and be enriched by our social existence. Clearly, some very critical and creative thinking about time is going to be essential, and this must include not only "working" time calculated as percentages of weeks or months, but also the way in which we interweave the time we allocate to our rights and responsibilities within our life-plans. One does not have to make a great leap in imagination to consider the beneficial effects such re-creative uses of time could have on our future aging populations, to say nothing of the individuals destined to join that currently oppressed group. However, it is impossible to believe that any such restructuring of our use of time can be contemplated or realized in the absence of a great deal of dialogue aimed at developing our critical thinking, educating us about the possibilities for change and fostering a will for and commitment to change. In addition and in concert, the social creation of such change would be dependent on the values upon which these changes would be predicated—in other words, those values and social relations that promote the realization of our full human potential.

I have a few other suggestions about re-thinking and re-creating democracy. Most of these we could begin to develop even within capitalist social relations, given the support of social democratic political leaders and parties. However, their full realization seems to me to be inextricably related to the re-creation of our use of time. Therefore, the *full* realization of some of these suggestions may be impossible in the absence of fundamental social change and transformation. Nevertheless, we can begin, even now, to place them within people's experiences, and as a consequence to put them on the political agenda and eventually move them to the top of all of our agendas for social transformation.

First, we need to develop more flexible concepts of which democratic forms (e.g., representative or direct democracy) are the most amenable, at least in the first instance, to the various sites of human practice. Academic or theoretical debates around the form of democracy tend to take an either/or direction. In most circles, the debate is caught within the framework of representative democracy and tends to focus on questions regarding the nature of the actual representatives (for an excellent analysis see Held, 1987). Should representatives be selected from the total range of citizens, or should they be selected only from those educated and cultured in a manner that "prepares" them for leadership or even those born and bred to lead? In radical circles, the arguments for forms of more direct democracy and the greater inclusion of many voices have been kept alive. As you know, I argue that all of us must be educated to have the critical and creative thinking necessary for good governance. I would also suggest that the form of democracy, at whatever level of civic life, must be rationally and democratically chosen on the basis of whether the form is consistent with achieving the best form of governance at that level. We could create overall democratic structures that interweave a variety of forms at all levels and even forms that are dynamic and, as a consequence, are responsive to historically specific circumstances and developments. This would require citizen flexibility or the willingness to participate to some degree all the time but to a greater degree at specific times.

My next suggestion has to do with developing a collective or communal concept of rights and responsibilities. In recent years in the United Kingdom, the idea of "rights" has been at the forefront of political discourse. However, rights have been decoupled too often from the idea of responsibility. In democracies, emphasis must be placed on both; however, to correct the current imbalance in emphasis, we also need to stress the rights, as well as the responsibilities, of citizens as a collective body rather than solely as individuals— which is the current emphasis. If we do not, then responsibility will continue to be individualized, and any individual "shortcomings" will be pathologized. The individuation of blame "creates" reactive democracy rather than the proactive democracy that I know we can create. By placing responsibility with communities or collectivities, we would foster and encourage dialogue and a much more democratic approach to decision-making and social transformation.

My final suggestion, for now, has to do with technology. A great deal of theorizing about democracy has assumed that more direct forms of democracy and citizen participation are impossible in complex societies. This has been especially the case in the twentieth century, when social entities have become both much larger and more complex. Had we not developed the technologies of telecommunications, albeit for different purposes, this stance might be difficult to refute. But it is refutable because the technology exists and the abilities to adapt it also exist. Current possibilities would allow democratic citizens—potentially all the people of the world—to communicate at long, even global, distances: to inform, debate, compromise (on the basis of hearing the other side rather than the abandonment of principle) and creatively engage in decision-making. Those who control our economic world are already linked by these technological innovations. There is no reason why we cannot utilize these achievements of human development to re-create democracy—to use them not only to interlink our political thinking and concerns but to integrate, or explicitly reintegrate, the political with the economic realms of our decision-making and popular democratic governance. Of course, we must have the will to do so, rather than only the ability to do this. The creation of such a will among the mass of people of our world will depend on social transformations wherein these ideas can be actively promoted, supported and experienced. This type of truly felt will for or commitment to alternative values can never be built by social engineering, but transformed social relations—created within transformative projects at whatever level or of whatever scope—can support such change. As you have read, I think the effort to transform our educational relations—whether in the classroom or in the context of other political, but equally educational, activities—is not only a beginning to but a necessary ingredient for authentic social transformation.

TRUTH

The idea that values, experience and knowledge have a potential resonance for all of humanity seems to have evaporated in what has been called our contemporary condition of postmodernity (Harvey, 1989). Therefore, concepts such as "truth" and "humanity" have lost all but very localized or particularistic significance. Relativism is the primary characteristic of many types of contemporary thought: that there are no truths, no universal values, is the "new truth" promulgated in celebration of human diversity. This celebration of diversity has been based on a simplistic recognition of difference, not a coming together to work through our diverse experiences in an attempt to establish a common or shared ground. As a consequence, any person or group's truth (i.e. explanations or observations of the real world) is just as legitimate as any other. When relativism is manifested in an extreme form, this is the result. However, it is only the scope and degree of this relativism that is "new" in our present historical experience of capitalist development.

Relativism in thought is a tendency that seems to arise and become more or less dominant during periods of capitalist crisis; therefore, it is a periodic tendency with a history that spans at least the last one hundred and fifty years (Hughes, 1959). However, when not operating in an extreme form, relativism has provided an important corrective, or the beginnings of a corrective, to the extremes of positivism which hold that "truth" can be discovered once and for all time by applying the "correct" scientific method to the study of reality. I go into more detail about this later when I discuss a radical concept of truth.

Some new features of relativism or its effects are emerging from the experience of the postmodern condition, features which if not challenged could mean the end of any possibility of transformative projects, critical praxis and the vision of a better future for the whole of humanity. These features run counter to objectives that have guided human striving for centuries. For example, they are completely contrary to the human quest to create a coherent self (Lovibond, 1989). The coherent self was a self or identity that individuals had to struggle to create, a lifelong project rather than a given or static condition. It was based on developing values and beliefs that were logically consistent and that were to help us make sense of our diverse experiences. These values and beliefs were not derived from individual whims or trivial aims. They were social values and beliefs that developed within and became valued within human social relations (Taylor, 1991). Radical social values developed within and informed historical struggles for freedom and the realization of a more fully human existence. For example, striving for the belief in "freedom of choice" only became a value in its own right because individuals could choose from and embrace values that were significant in terms of both the social good and the individual's fulfilment.

The contemporary experience of relativism and the fragmentation of our existence has been accompanied by the loss of the concept of social significance (pp. 25–41), or its relocation only in particularized experiences. For example, individuals may still value "freedom of choice" in the creation of their identities, but the choice is frequently made from a collage of fragments. Other than the value of diversity, there is nothing left of broad social significance to provide a coherence to the self that is created. The proponents of this "kaleidoscopic self" express no sense of loss, but surely there is a loss. On one hand, what possible reason can there be for transformative vision and efforts or critical praxis if we accept the "death of the coherent self," the "death of the subject," the impossibility of people creatively and critically engaged in creating the present and future? Indeed, what reason would there be for promoting critical intelligence or critical thinking? People do not need to be critical thinkers, or even intelligent, to live in and to adapt to a fragmented world, within fragmented identities, where the only task is to satisfy individual wants and desires and to establish the "right" to do so. All people need to do is to succumb to the intoxication of the marketplace, the world of capitalist commodities, and to create life-styles and "cultures" from these previously commodified or processed raw materials. Clearly, there is more at stake here than just the values and objectives of those working for social transformation, the humanization of our existence. The very meaning of being human or of realizing our human potential is also at stake. Throughout human history, there always has been the possibility that people might uncritically choose to become less human, as well as the alternative possibility of people critically choosing to become more fully human. Radical social transformation must be grounded in and must foster the latter alternative. To assist us in this, we need to develop a radical concept of truth.

We need a concerted challenge to the current relativization of truth. To engage in this challenge, we will need to distinguish clearly between a dialectical/radical concept of truth and other, ultimately conservative enlightenment concepts of truth. The latter focus solely on universal, transhistorical, static or infinite truths, the notions of truth promulgated within the extremes of positivism.

To challenge relativism and distinguish our critical concept of truth from positivism, we need to search for four types of truth that are valuable only in relation to one another. Also, in our dialogues with others we need to be clear about which type we are discussing. This is how I conceptualize these four types of truth. First, there are some truths that, thus far, seem to hold across the entirety of human history—for example, human beings, for better or worse, create history. These could be called *meta-transhistorical truths*; they must always be tested, but it is difficult to think that it could ever be otherwise. Then there are truths that hold across history to date, but we can envision that it could be otherwise—for example, human beings, all of us, make history, but so far this is not a history based on the critical choice of the majority of human beings. It has been a history primarily created out of reproductive rather than critical praxis. This is a *transhistorical truth*. This need not be the truth for the future. Third, there are truths that pertain to the foundation of a particular social formation. They are *historically specific* to and necessary for the continued survival of a social form—for example, exploitation within capitalism rests on the social relations between "free" wage labor and capital. Finally, within any social form there are *conjuncturally specific truths*—for example, currently, capitalist enterprises are using multiple or "flexible" ways of exploiting labor and accumulating capital and doing so to a greater degree than ever before. This is referred to as capitalist restructuring within the regime of flexible accumulation (Harvey, 1989).

When taken together, these four types of truth constitute the dialectical concept of truth that we will need to challenge current concepts and to engage in authentic projects for social transformation.

EQUALITY

Even in my early teens, I had become a passionate devotee to the ideal of equality. Having been born in the United States and then educated there, I had witnessed far too many examples of gross inequalities but was also constantly exposed to and inculcated with liberal democratic principles based on the ideal of equality. I was a critic of the inequalities, especially the experience of them, and still am, but, at that time, I did not question or think critically about the actual concept of equality that I had long championed. When I first moved to Britain, which was just after the introduction of the comprehensive school and during a time when the philosophy of comprehensive schooling and antistreaming debates were prominent within education and political discourse, I naively thought I had found a much more egalitarian society or at least one where people were more aware of the problems and were striving to overcome them. It took a few years to lose the naivety and a few more to begin to question the liberal democratic concept of equality which I prized so highly.

As is normally the case, experience provided the first doubts. However, I shall always be indebted to Stuart Hall (especially Hall, 1982) for initiating a critical challenge to my thinking about equality. Within his critique of liberal democratic ideology, it becomes clear that many of our democratic principles, especially equality, can operate only on a highly formal or abstract level. Whereas many of us may believe that they should be realized in our daily experience, perhaps we should be questioning whether these principles were ever intended to operate in our material experiences and whether they possibly could do so within capitalist social relations. Raising these questions led me to even more profound questions and many doubts about the ideal of equality. Once again, my thinking was challenged and then aided by the writings of Karl Marx. I go into more detail about this later. First, I want to examine some doubts and confusions that pertain in the contemporary use of the concept of equality.

The first is a doubt that must be explored in depth within our discussions about social transformation. It seems to me that any specific concept of equality depends on the actual existence of inequality and various oppressions. Since, as I have argued, consciousness and our concepts come from " social being," I must question whether we will need or use the concept of "equality" once we abolish the negative experiences that have led to its creation.

We also need to be aware of and think critically about the present confusion and logically contradictory nature of many struggles for equality. Most people in the United Kingdom and many other countries profess a belief in equal opportunities; however, some people see these as ends in themselves, whereas others profess them as a means of achieving equal outcomes. Obviously, these two groups of individuals have very different specific concepts of equality and very different goals for the present and future of humanity. The first group simply desire, in the quest for fairness, that everyone has an equal chance to participate in a system, be it an educational, political or civic one. Their goals can be equated to "access" and therefore their concept of equality, although more materially based than abstract or formal concepts, is reducible to access to the given system. Those who profess equality of opportunity as a means to equality of outcome seem to adhere to a range of ideas regarding the ideal of equality of outcome. Some seem to think that people can emerge from or participate within any system sharing the same status and, even in the case of employment, the same incomes. They have a more radical concept of fairness but frequently seem to ignore how contradictory this value is within capitalist social relations which depend upon the values of competition and meritocracy. Others more willingly acknowledge that equality of outcome can be achieved only within totally transformed social relations of production and exchange. However, neither of these groups, who promote the ideal of equality of outcome, questions whether "equality" is the ideal that we should be striving to manifest in our social existence.

For the present I must hang on to a concept of equality; however, although I do not have an exact qualifier to express it, I think that it is a qualitatively different concept and one that I hope will be discussed and debated within projects for social transformation. For now, I call it alternatively equality of appreciation, recognition, value or worth. It is a concept of equality which has to do with how we relate to both other human beings and how we perceive ourselves and to the transformed social relations that we might strive to create. My concept has developed from reading Karl Marx but is perhaps best summed up by Freire's (1974) words: "I can not be unless you are."

Marx first challenged my thinking about equality when I read his "Critique of the Gotha Programme" (Marx, 1875). I referred to this piece in chapter 2 but I think it deserves repeating. Marx was critiquing a supposedly socialist program that he evaluated as being little more than a struggle for access to capitalist forms of democracy, and he was challenging his German comrades to consider how little of real importance had been realized through such struggles. He goes on to consider the idea that economic equality can be established according to the amount of labor time that each worker expends. He challenges this ideal on the basis of the fact that it can only be based on a quantitative, rather than a qualitative, measure—the former being the basis, he argues, of every right. He also argues that this presents a very one-sided and limited view of human beings. He says that we are not the same and should not be equated on the basis of some narrow measure that renders us the same. If we were the same, we would not be different individuals, Marx argues, and because of this he then goes on to promulgate a very important principle of and goal for social transformation: "[F]rom each according to [their] ability to each according to [their] need!" (p. 569).

Marx was able to challenge my thinking about equality with his analysis and words in this source because I had previously read something in his early works which has always moved me very deeply and which enabled me to understand what he was proposing in this much later critique. I have quoted it in chapter 2 but will repeat it here in the hope that it challenges you, in the same way it has me, to think about equality, and also difference. As I said above, my concept of equality has to do with how we relate to human beings. This quotation begins with a brief statement about our current relations and then goes on to offer a beautiful vision of how we could relate to one another within transformed humanized social relations.

Our mutual value is for us the value of our mutual products. Thus, [human beings themselves are] for us mutually worthless.

Supposing we had produced in a human manner, each of us would in [our] production have doubly affirmed [ourselves] and [our] fellow [human beings]. I would have: (1) objectified in my production my individuality and its peculiarity and thus both in my activity enjoyed the individual expression of my life and also in looking at the object have had the individual pleasure of realizing that my personality was objective, visible to the senses, and thus a power raised beyond doubt. (2) In your enjoyment or use of my product I would have had the direct enjoyment of realizing that I had both satisfied a human need by my work and also objectified the human essence and therefore fashioned for another human being the object

> that met his [her] need. (3) I would have been for you the mediator between you and the species and thus been acknowledged and felt by you a completion of your own essence and as a necessary part of yourself and have thus realized that I am confirmed both in your thought and in your love. (4) In my expression of my life I would have fashioned your expression of your life, and thus in my own activity have realized my own essence, my human, my communal essence.
>
> In that case our products would be like so many mirrors, out of which our essence shone.
>
> Thus, in this relationship what occurred on my side would also occur on yours. [Marx, 1844, pp. 121–22]

The remainder of this citation is a summary of what he has said, and I urge you to read it.

These words and the "Gotha Critique" compelled me to rethink my concept of equality and to reflect more deeply on what I appreciate in life and always have. People, often personal or student friends, who bring to my experience different perspectives and experiences, enrich my life especially when they challenge me to think again about my own thinking and in so doing to either change or become clearer about why I think as I do. When we share our differences within dialogue, listening carefully to one another and helping each other to examine the origins of our thinking, we usually come to a sharing of values and commitments, and the process that has led to this means that what we share really means something significant. Even when we do not reach a consensus on a particular occasion, the dialogical process helps us keep our minds open and questioning, enabling us to be curious and reflective about our developing, critical consciousness. To me, this is a necessary condition for or part of becoming more fully human. Because of my experience, it is impossible for me to think that there is any type of work that contributes to human society which is more valuable than any other. We can be rich in needs and are rich in the abilities to meet these needs. If we could share this valuing, we would become more amenable to sharing in the more arduous work, thus freeing all of us to engage in a rich variety of work and contributions to human society as well as the development of our particular individualities.

Where do the ideas in this chapter, and throughout this book, leave us? My intention was to try to initiate a dialogue that might bring about the vision and hope that we can engage in authentic social transformation that could humanize our existence. I also tried to introduce some of the analysis that we will need to bring our hopes and visions to fruition. Only you can be the judge of whether these intentions have been realized.

I have only one final comment to make. The structure of our language sometimes prevents me from expressing my points dialectically. Often, as in the book's structure, these must be expressed in a way that suggests a sequence—that is,vision then analysis. I am reminded of a quote from Gramsci that I treasure and often use:

> An historic act can only be performed [collectively], and this presupposes the attainment of a "cultural-social" unity through which a multiplicity of dispersed wills, with heterogeneous aims, are welded together with a single aim, on the basis of an equal and common conception of the world, both general and particular, . . . where the intellectual base is so well rooted, assimilated and experienced that it becomes passion (*SPN*, p. 349).

Gramsci's words can also be interpreted sequentially. First, we need the intellectual base, then we develop the passion. I do not think that this was his intended meaning, any more than it is mine. Visions and passions must develop in concert, in an intimate dance, with analysis and intellect. Only then will we create the possibilities for authentic, humanizing, revolutionary social transformations.

REFERENCES

Bowles, S., and Gintis, H. (1986). *Democracy and Capitalism*. London: Routledge and Kegan Paul.

Freire, P. (1972). *Pedagogy of the Oppressed*. Harmondsworth: Penguin.

Freire, P. (1974). *Authority versus Authoritarianism*. Audiotape in the series "Thinking with Paulo Freire." Sydney, Australia: Australian Council of Churches.

Gramsci, A. (1971). *Selections from the Prison Notebooks of Antonio Gramsci*, edited and translated by Q. Hoare and G. N. Smith. London: Lawrence and Wishart.

Hall, S. (1982). "Managing Conflict, Producing Consent." Unit 21, in Block 5: *Conformity, Consensus and Conflict, D102 Social Sciences: A Foundation Course*. Milton Keynes: Open University Press.

Harvey, D. (1989). *The Condition of Postmodernity*. London: Blackwell.

Held, D. (1987). *Models of Democracy*. Cambridge: Polity Press.

Hughes, H. S. (1959). *Consciousness and Society*. London: MacGibbon and Kee.

Lovibond, S. (1989). "Feminism and Postmodernism." *New Left Review*, No. 178 (November/December), 5–28.

Marx, K. (1844). "On James Mill." In D. McLellan (Ed.), *Karl Marx: Selected Writings*. Oxford: Oxford University Press, 1977.

Marx, K. (1875). "Critique of the Gotha Programme." In D. McLellan (Ed.), *Karl Marx: Selected Writings*. Oxford: Oxford University Press, 1977.

Taylor, C. (1991). *The Ethics of Authenticity*. Cambridge: Harvard University Press.

Further Readings

Allman, P. (1987). "Paulo Freire's Educational Approach: A Struggle for Meaning." In G. Allen et al. (Eds.), *Community Education: An Agenda for Reform* (pp. 214–237). Milton Keynes: Open University Press.

Allman, P. (1988). "Gramsci, Freire, and Illich: Their Contributions to Education for Socialism." In T. Lovett (Ed.), *Radical Approaches to Adult Education: A Reader* (pp. 85–1 13). London: Routledge.

Allman, P. (1994). "Paulo Freire's Contributions to Radical Adult Education." *Studies in the Education of Adults*, *26*, No. 2, 144–161.

Allman, P., and Wallis, J. (1990). "Praxis: Implications for 'Really' Radical Education." *Studies in the Education of Adults*, *22*, No. 1 (April), 14–30.

Allman, P., and Wallis, J. (1995a). "Challenging the Post Modern Condition: Radical Adult Education for Critical Intelligence." In M. Mayo and J. Thompson (Eds.), *Adult Learning. Critical Intelligence and Social Change* (pp. 18–33). Leicester: National Institute of Continuing Education.

Allman, P., and Wallis, J. (1995b). "Gramsci's Challenge to the Politics of the Left in 'Our Times.'" *International Journal of Lifelong Education*, *14*, No. 2 (March–April), 120–143.

Anderson, P. (1980). *Arguments Within English Marxism*. London: Verso.

Callinicos, A. (1998). "The Secret of the Dialectic." *International Socialism* (Spring), 93–103.

Freire, P. (1978). *Pedagogy in Process: The Letters to Guinea-Bissau.* New York: Continuum.

Freire, P., (1994). *Pedagogy of Hope: Reliving Pedagogy of the Oppressed.* New York: Continuum.

Freire, P., and Faundez, A. (1989). *Learning to Question, A Pedagogy of Liberation.* Geneva: World Council of Churches.

Freire, P., and Macedo, D. (1987). *Literacy: Reading the Word and the World.* London: Routledge and Kegan Paul.

Giroux, H. A. (1981). *Ideology. Culture and the Process of Schooling.* London: Falmer.

Giroux, H. A. (1992). *Border Crossings: Cultural Workers and the Politics of Education.* London: Routledge and Kegan Paul.

Giroux, H. A., and Freire, P. (1987). "Series Introduction." In D. W. Livingstone et al., *Critical Pedagogy and Cultural Power* (pp. xi–xvi). London: Macmillan.

Gramsci, A. (1977). *Selections from Political Writings 1910–1920,* selected and edited by Quinton Hoare, translated by John Matthews. London: Lawrence and Wishart.

Gramsci, A. (1979). *Letters from Prison,* translated and with an Introduction by L. Lawner. London: Quartet Books.

Gramsci, A. (1994). *Pre-Prison Writings,* edited by R. Bellamy, translated by V. Cox. Cambridge: Cambridge University Press.

Hall, S. (1978). "The Hinderland of Science: Ideology and the Sociology of Knowledge." In Centre for Contemporary Cultural Studies, *On Ideology.* London: Hutchinson.

Harman, C. (1984). *Explaining the Crisis.* London: Bookmarks.

Harman, C. (1996). "Globalisation: A Critique of a New Orthodoxy." *International Socialism,* No. 73 (Winter), 2–33.

Holloway, J. (1994). "Global Capital and the Nation State." *Capital and Class, 52* (Spring), 23–49.

Jacoby, R. (1977). *Social Amnesia.* London: Harvester.

Jacoby, R. (1981). *Dialectic of Defeat: Contours of Western Marxism.* London: Cambridge University Press.

Kosík, K. (1976). *Dialectic of the Concrete.* Dordrecht: Reidel.

Larrain, J. (1983). *Marxism and Ideology.* London: Macmillan.

Larrain, J. (1979). *The Concept of Ideology.* London: Hutchinson.

Mayo, P. (1994). "Synthesizing Gramsci and Freire: Possibilities for a Theory of Radical Education." *International Journal of Lifelong Education, 13,* No. 2 (March–April), 125–148.

Mayo, P. (1993). "When Does It Work? Freire's Pedagogy in Context." *Studies in the Education of Adults, 25,* No. 1 (April), 11–30.

Mayo, P. (1996). "Transformative Adult Education in the Age of Globalisation: A Gramscian–Freirean Synthesis and Beyond." *Alberta Journal of Educational Research*, *42*, No. 2 (June), 148–160.

McLaren, P., and Lankshear, C. (Eds.) (1994). *Politics of Liberation: Paths from Freire*. London: Routledge.

McLaren, P., and Leonard, P. (Eds.) (1993). *Paulo Freire: A Critical Encounter*. London: Routledge.

McLellan, D. (1979). *Marxism after Marx*. London: Macmillan.

Peet, R. (1991). *Global Capitalism: Theories of Societal Development*. London: Routledge.

Ransome, P. (1992). *Antonio Gramsci: A New Introduction*. London: Harvester Wheatsheaf.

Thompson, J. L. (1983). *Learning Liberation: Women's Response to Men's Education*. London: Croom Helm.

Wainwright, H. (1994). *Arguments for a New Left: Answering the Free Market Right*. London: Blackwell.

Wood, Meiksins, E. (1988). "Capitalism and Human Emancipation." *New Left Review*, No. 167 (January/February), 3–20.

Wood, Meiksins, E. (1995). *Democracy against Capitalism*. Cambridge: Cambridge University Press.

Index

ABOUT THE AUTHOR

Paula Allman is an Honorary Research Fellow in the School of Continuing Education at the University of Nottingham, England.

36687703R00103

Printed in Great Britain
by Amazon